HOW

WR

A WILL

& GAIN PROBATE

HOW TO
WRITE
A WILL
& GAIN PROBATE

ALL YOU NEED TO DO IT YOURSELF

10TH EDITION

MARLENE GARSIA

**KOGAN
PAGE**

First published in 1989
Second edition 1992
Third edition 1993
Fourth edition 1993
Fifth edition 1995
Sixth edition 1996
Seventh edition 1997
Eighth edition 1998
Ninth edition 1999
Tenth edition 2000

Readers should check before taking irrevocable action in case of changes to the law.

While every care has been taken to ensure the accuracy of the contents of this work, no responsibility for loss occasioned to any person acting or refraining from action as a result of any statement in it can be accepted by the Author. Amendments have been made following the Chancellor's Budget Statement on 21 March 2000. However, Parliament still has to agree to these changes and it is therefore possible that the legislation will be further amended after this edition has gone to press. Readers should be aware of this and obtain details of any late amendments.

Kogan Page Limited
120 Pentonville Road
London N1 9JN

British Library Cataloguing in Publication Data

A CIP record for this book is available from the British Library.

ISBN 0 7494 3317 5

Typeset by Saxon Graphics Ltd, Derby
Printed and bound in Great Britain by Bell & Bain Ltd, Glasgow

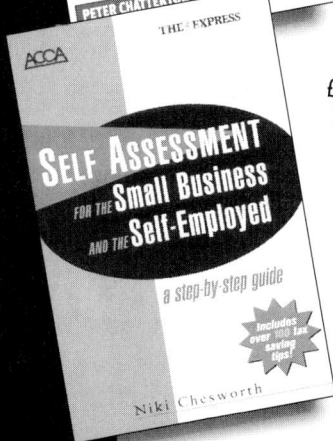

Aid for the Aged in Distress

Financial relief for distressed elderly people throughout the United Kingdom

Aid for the Aged in Distress is a specialist national 'no frills' charity. It is concerned with frail, elderly people who are facing immediate financial hardship or distress because their urgent needs cannot be met adequately from resources available through family support or by statutory and voluntary services.

The general aim is to help sustain people in their homes by making relevant personal grants as a contribution to the cost of necessary equipment or other exceptional expenditure. Most frequent examples of assistance would include:-

HEATING

Warmth is a comfort to us all. To the elderly it can be a matter of life or death. Hypothermia kills.

TELEPHONE AND ALARMS

Without a 'phone, many elderly people are isolated. Where there is no local authority support, installation costs can be beyond the means of many.

CLOTHING

In a cold winter, warm clothing is an essential for life. Without it, body heat is lost and Hypothermia threatens once again.

BEDDING

For us all, bed is a place of warmth and comfort. To many elderly it is simply the safest place to be. Adequate and warm bedding is an essential.

ESSENTIAL FURNITURE

With constant use, everything eventually wears out. A bed with a broken spring, an armchair from which it is increasingly difficult to get up from, saucepans with insecure handles, worn out and dangerous appliances.

Aid for the Aged in Distress does not receive a penny from the State or local government resources and relies solely on the generosity of supporters to continue its services. It is willing to receive applications directly from elderly people, or, more usually, from individuals or agencies acting on their behalf. The aim is always to process applications promptly, recognising that it is probably being made as a last resort in difficult circumstances.

With the increasing numbers of elderly people we desperately need your help with donations, covenants or legacies. Please help us not to let them down.

WITNESS THE WILL WITH WHICH WE WORK

Aid for the Aged in Distress
Room WW, 54 London Road, Morden, Surrey SM4 5BE
Tel: 020 8640 5523 Fax: 020 8640 9163
email: *agedistres@aol.com*
website: *www.agedistress.org.uk*

Contents

Acknowledgements   xiii

Foreword   xix

Introduction   1

1. **Why Do You Need a Will?**   10
   Who can make a will? 15; Decide on your aims 16;
   How much will my estate be worth in, say, 20 years'
   time? 18; Understanding the jargon 18

2. **What Happens If You Die Without a Valid Will?**   27
   Present rules 27

3. **What You Should Know Before Writing a Will**   34
   What is termed as 'property'? 34; Financial matters 35;
   What is an executor? Who can be appointed? 39;
   Where should a will be kept? 40; What is a trust? 41;
   Small estates in England and Wales 43; 'Excepted
   estates' 43; What is a life interest? 45

4. **What Can Affect Your Will?**   47
   Marriage 47; Divorce 48; Revocation of a will 48;
   A 'wish of intent' 49; Disputes and unknown factors 49;
   Making a gift void 51; Rules to follow 52

Contents

5. **How To Write a Will**   55
   Checklist for your will 55; Example of a will 61;
   Notes 63; What is a codicil? 66

6. **A Question of Tax**   68
   Equalization of estates 70; Settlements 72; Transfers
   between husband and wife 73; Domicile 74; Gifts 74;
   When is inheritance tax applied? 76; What can be
   achieved if no prior planning has been done? 77;
   Business property relief 79; Relief for successive
   charges 80; Related property rules 80; Disposing of
   an asset 82; Interest in possession trusts 83; Children:
   accumulation and maintenance settlements 84;
   Discretionary trusts 85; Jointly owned property 85;
   How is tax paid? 86; Insurance against inheritance
   tax 88

7. **Dealing With Personal Tax Matters After Death**   89
   Allowable expenses before inheritance tax 90; How
   does this affect the surviving partner's tax position?
   91; Self-assessment 92; What is a tax code? 94;
   Income tax due during the period of administration 94;
   The distribution of income to a beneficiary 96

8. **Who Can You Go To For Help?**   99
   When will you need assistance? 99; Where do you
   start? 100; Solicitors 101; The Probate Registry 103;
   Probate Registries and their local Probate
   Offices 105; Where else can advice be sought? 108

9. **Documentation**   110
   Death certificate 110; What is a grant and why is it
   necessary? 111; What are all these forms for? 111

10. **Valuing and Administering the Estate**   114
    How to start 115; Property 116; National Savings
    certificates 120; Premium Bonds 120; Insurance 121;
    Bank and building society accounts 122; Shares and
    other investments 123; Other income 126; Hire
    purchase 126; Listing the valuations 127;
    Administering a trust 128

11. **What Happens in Scotland?**   130
What is a 'small estate'? 130; Rights 132; Estate
checklist 133; What does it all mean? 134;
Children 135; Heritable property 136; Intestate
estate 138; Does divorce alter a will? 138; Debts 138;
Useful addresses 139

12. **Winding Up an Estate**   140
Property 140; Bookkeeping 144; Tax returns 146;
Accounts 150; Distributing legacies 150; Final
accounts 152; Capital accounts 152;
The closing stages 154

Appendix 1   **Probate Checklist**   157
Appendix 2   **Probate Fees Payable by a Personal**
                   Applicant in England and Wales   159

Index   161

Index of Advertisers   169

Have you the will
to change their lives for the better?

Loneliness, despair, homelessness, hunger - maybe all they need is a little love.
Sadly, today so many people, both young and old are in such a desperate situation
they need something a little more practical. Like a bed. Help with the shopping.
A chat. Or just a welcoming cup of tea.

Every week, The Salvation Army cares for more than 60,000 people in the
UK alone. We don't apportion blame, we don't moralise. We just roll our
sleeves up and get on with it.

By leaving a legacy to The Salvation Army in your will you are doing more than
helping us in our vital work, you are sowing a seed of kindness for people
desperately in need.

To find out how you can leave a legacy to The Salvation Army, please write to us at our new address:
The Salvation Army, UK Territory, Fundraising Department, 101 Newington Causeway, London SE1 6BN.
Or call 0171 367 4800, quoting reference number LMGP1.

Thank you and God bless you.
The Salvation Army is a registered charity.
www.salvationarmy.org.uk

MAKE YOUR WILL, MAKE THEIR LIVES.

Acknowledgements

I would like to thank all those who have helped me in writing this book, in particular: Chris Marsh, Registrar, Birmingham Probate Registry; Miss Eilidh Scobbie of Burnett and Reid for reading the chapter 'What Happens in Scotland?'; and Hills and Co for the two chapters on taxation.

BRITISH UNION FOR THE ABOLITION OF VIVISECTION (BUAV)
16a Crane Grove, London N7 8NN
Telephone: 020 7700 4888

For over 100 years, the BUAV has led the campaign to end animal experiments through the use of high profile campaigns and educational activities. Working strictly within the law, we undertake many ambitious campaigns and investigations both nationally and internationally to expose the cruel and senseless treatment of animals.

The BUAV's work has not only gained widespread media attention and public support but has resulted in real victories against animal suffering. For example, in 1998, after 12 years of hard BUAV campaigning, the Government announced a full ban on cosmetic testing in the UK. This announcement saw a whole class of animal experiments disappear.

In fact, every time our investigators carry out their undercover work, we gain more and more evidence to show that the use of animals in experiments is both shameful and needless. For example, last July the BUAV, with the help of the Daily Mail, launched its most recent campaign against Harlan UK, the biggest breeder of beagle dogs for the research industry in the United Kingdom. BUAV exposed the cruelty of over breeding and the destruction of surplus dogs as well as the shocking living conditions. There was a public outcry and as a result the Home Office launched its own inquiry into Harlan, which is still ongoing. By getting the public and government to take action as a result of our findings, the end to animal suffering is brought one step closer.

It is therefore vital that our important work continues. Your gift of a legacy would give us the financial security to continue these investigations and help keep the pressure on those companies and governments who are still involved in animal exploitation. Please give your support in this way and help us to end the misery and suffering of laboratory animals once and for all.

If you would like to receive further information on the BUAV, please write or telephone Mr J W Fenwick-Smith at the above contact details.

Wood Green Animal Shelters

Wood Green Animal Shelters has cared for homeless, abandoned and mistreated animals for over 75 years, since its foundation in 1924. The shelters, in Cambridgeshire, Hertfordshire and North London, aim to provide the best possible care for the thousands of animals taken in each year, and to find them new homes wherever possible.

Many pet owners worry about what will happen when they die, or are unable to continue to care for their animals. The Wood Green **Pet Alert Scheme** has been developed in response to this concern. Registration costs nothing and offers peace of mind to caring owners, especially if they are elderly or living alone.

The charity could not continue its work without the kindness of people supporting us through donations and legacies. By remembering us in their Will, people can help secure a better future for their pets and thousands of other animals in need.

Wood Green Animal Shelters
King's Bush Farm, London Road
Godmanchester,
Cambridgeshire PE18 8LJ
Tel:01480 830014; Fax: 01480 830158
Website: www.woodgreen.org.uk
Registered Charity No. 298348

SSAFA FORCES Help

Yesterday, today and tomorrow,

We're there for them

If you would like to make a donation or find out more about our activities, please contact our Central Office:

SSAFA Forces Help, 19 Queen Elizabeth Street, London SE1 2LP
Telephone: 020 7403 8783 Fax: 020 7403 8815
email: public-awareness@ssafa-forces-help.org.uk
www.ssafa-forces-help.org.uk

The Soldiers, Sailors, Airmen and Families Association - Forces Help

Registered Charity No. 210760 Established 1885.

CSG/00

Committed for life

SSAFA Forces Help is committed to helping anyone who has served just one paid day in any of our three Armed Forces, including the Reserves - and their dependants: spouses, children, widows and widowers.

Our help knows no diplomatic or economic boundaries - wherever in the world, someone with a UK Service connection finds themselves in need, we can reach them.

Today, there are more than 7,500 volunteers working from branches and committees nation wide and overseas, helping the serving and ex-Service communities. The huge growth in the professional side of the Association's work is proof of the experience we have amassed and the respect in which that is held.

In any one year, our voluntary and professional staff help more than 100,00 people.

It is important that growth does not compromise quality. Recruitment of the right people and their training is essential to the results we achieve in such a wide range of roles.

Our current role

Whilst we are often referred to as a 'Service charity', our priority is people: people who choose a life in the Services, whether Regular or Volunteer Reserve, both whilst they are serving and after they have left. Our commitment is to support them with practical and emotional help when they find themselves in need. Helping families is a major part of our work, but we are equally committed to helping single people.

We also offer a professional social work service to the serving community in the UK and we provide health services to overseas commands. We represent the best interests of the people we aim to help by acting as advisers to the Ministry of Defence, in our fields of expertise.

Formal 'charters' reflect the guiding principles which are common to both the voluntary and professional arms of the Association. We pledge to respect people's dignity, to treat them in a compassionate, impartial way and to deal in confidence with any information entrusted to staff or volunteers. Whilst people's needs vary, it is SSAFA Forces Help's commitment to approach each problem with the same integrity and each individual with the same consideration.

For further information about how you can help us, whether it be making a donation, making a bequest or becoming a volunteer, please see our advertisement below.

British Trust for Ornithology

Room 110C, The Nunnery, Thetford, Norfolk. IP24 2PU

Tel: 01842 750050 Fax: 01842 750030

Registered Charity No. 216652   Registered in England and Wales No. 357284

There are over 7,000 keen Garden BirdWatch members who record the common birds in their gardens throughout the year. They provide vital information on the ups and downs of our common birds. For more information on how to take part in Garden BirdWatch, contact Jacky Prior at the address above.

The British Trust for Ornithology is the leading research organisation studying the UK's birds and their habitats. Since 1933, tens of thousands of BTO volunteers have monitored the bird populations throughout the UK. The unique partnership of fieldworkers, survey organisers and scientists, based at our Thetford headquarters, enables the BTO to shape the future of bird conservation throughout the country and beyond.

Foreword

Despite the recent publicity encouraging individuals to make wills, the majority of people still do not do so. The reasons given are many and varied. But it means that over 64,000 letters of administration are issued each year to relatives or friends of the deceased, simply because the deceased failed to make a will.

It may be that a visit to a solicitor is thought costly, which at present it is not. For solicitors often do deals whereby wills can be made for £40 or £50 a person, well below their normal charge-out rates. However, should they be named as an executor their normal hourly charge would apply and this would be more expensive unless you negotiate a fixed price for dealing with probate. Of course, this is difficult as we do not know the precise time of our demise. Using a solicitor does not mean that all matters will go smoothly and that the wording in the will will be without dispute. There have been occasions when the wording in a will completed by a solicitor has been such that it has caused a dispute.

You do not, however, have to seek professional help. A 'Do-It-Yourself' approach, provided it is done carefully, can quite adequately be carried out by an inexperienced person. This applies both to writing your will and to dealing with probate matters for a deceased relative or friend. Indeed, if you are the residuary beneficiary of a will, it would also be more profitable to deal with the probate yourself through the Personal Applications Department of your nearest Probate Registry, than to pay professional charges, which start at between £70 and £80 per hour but can be £90 to £120 per hour, sometimes more. A 'Do-It-Yourself' approach has many benefits, as you will see as you read this book. But it will prove very difficult emotionally should you be proving the estate of a partner. The period of grieving can be accentuated time and time again when dealing with your loved one's affairs. For this reason, you would be well advised to consider using the services of a solicitor or to rely on a fellow executor.

This book has been written for most people, from those who want to know but do not know whom to ask to those who still have questions, perhaps simply about the value of their estate. It has been written by a layperson for a layperson. And it has been written in plain English with as little use of legalistic words and phrases as the text will allow. The book is a practical and basic guide on how to write a will and gain probate. After all, it is a subject that touches all our lives at one time or another!

In researching this book it has become clear that, under English law, provided an estate is relatively straightforward, complicated trusts are not involved, and extensive estate planning is not needed, then there is nothing to stop the individual from handling his or her relation's affairs – whatever the size of the estate. Despite this, only a minority of people do so.

Scotland is another matter. I have explained briefly the position in Scotland, dealing with small estates, the differences when writing a will and gaining confirmation. The information given is not exhaustive since in Scotland solicitors' help is often required by the authorities. The level of assistance is not available to the same degree as that found in England and Wales, nor do matters appear as straightforward – except for processing small estates.

The appropriate authorities both in England and Scotland have been extremely helpful, as they would be to any person seeking their assistance.

I have started at the very beginning, with what I would have to do myself when writing a will and working on from that point.

This book has been written sequentially, step by step, so that readers can clearly follow what to do next whether writing their own will, planning their estate or acting as executors carrying out their obligations on behalf of a deceased friend or relative. Frequently asked questions are answered. How do you write your own will? What makes a will invalid? Who can be called upon to deal with an estate? Where do you find your nearest Probate Registry? What happens if you die without making a will?

Family responsibilities necessitate family and financial decisions. How do you best ensure that your children's inheritance is not taken away by the tax inspector? What options are available when arranging your affairs? Is insurance the answer?

The readers who use this book will find it helpful in all relevant aspects. It is not meant as a bible in which all possible questions are asked and answered. However, you can take heart, as you will find no unexplained text to baffle you, merely straightforward information as to what needs to be done and how to do it.

Recently a friend has had to prove his late father's estate. His comment was: 'I had no idea it would have been as easy as it has been.'

Introduction

Everyone at some time or another finds themselves faced with making arrangements following the death of a loved one, whether a relative or close friend. At this distressing time, any mention of a will (much less the proving of it), or what assets the deceased owned, will be seen as an intrusion into personal grief, indeed an invasion of privacy at a time when you feel least able to cope.

This book cannot help in alleviating the suffering that will be felt with the loss of a loved one – dealing with grief is a very individual matter. What it can do is to provide information about what will be needed and what matters have to be dealt with in as straightforward and uncomplicated a manner as the subject allows. It tells you what to do and why, and how to go about it. It takes a step-by-step view of the necessary procedures from writing a will to estate planning and proving a will.

The first part of the book will be concerned with how to write a will. Basically you 'make' a will because you want to direct who receives your assets following your death. Occasionally, you may even want to ensure that certain people do not receive a share in your estate. You may have already made your will either with the help of a solicitor or on a standard proprietary will form available from most large newsagents. However, if you have not done either, then it is a matter that must be considered as an urgent task. If you have already made out a will, as your personal situations change it may become necessary to write a new will.

The time period over which this can be done varies but any major change such as marriage, inheritance, death or divorce should necessitate a revised will.

Examples of a basic will and specific clauses which may be added in different circumstances are also to be found. How to make an addition to your will (a *codicil*) is also shown.

Approximately one in every five persons writes their own

will. In London the number is higher, one in every three, while in Scotland the figure is approximately one in every four. However, most people still go to a solicitor, not because their affairs are complex but because they do not know where to start or find the task daunting.

Estate planning and inheritance tax are examined in Chapter 6. For the inexperienced this subject can be not only bewildering but frightening too.

At the end of Chapter 8 the local offices of the Probate Registry in England and Wales are listed. These offices are the first place to start. For the addresses in Scotland, see Chapter 11.

Scottish law differs in many ways from the law of England and Wales. These differences are noted separately in Chapter 11.

Within the limitations of this book, the basic differences for both making and proving a will (and for obtaining confirmation in Scotland) are defined and clarified. However, should any complication arise then do seek professional advice.

Naturally, if your affairs are complicated with, perhaps, the existence of a trust fund, an existing business or other external factors which affect the estate, then the best person to go to would be a solicitor. Solicitors are experts not only in drawing up wills but trust funds too, and can act as executors of an estate. You may feel that your estate would benefit from tax planning and therefore it is important to go and see your tax adviser. They may suggest a Potentially Exempt Transfer (PET) whereby you gift certain investments or belongings to say your grandchildren via a Trust. Your tax adviser would then discuss the drawing up of this document with your solicitor. However, do be aware that these services have to be paid for. A solicitor's fee was previously based on the value of the estate (and some practices still use this as a guide) but now it refers to the length of time (and expenses too) taken to handle your affairs. This will be based on an hourly charge, starting at circa £85 per hour (although there are some solicitors who charge £120 or more per hour) plus disbursements, ie expenses. In addition, there is an administration cost in the form of a charge for letters received and letters sent, and these are circa £4 and £12 each, respectively.

Without your help, this is the only legacy for Britain's Wildlife

Hunting with dogs is a legacy of cruelty that's been handed down for generations.

Foxes, deer and hares are the defenceless victims, chased by hunters and hounds, then savaged to death.

For fun.

But one thing could eradicate the terrible legacy of bloodsports.

A legacy from you.

By leaving part of your estate to the League Against Cruel Sports, you'll be providing vital funds for our campaign to abolish these barbaric acts.

Pledging a legacy is easy. Simply write to Rebecca Yates, Legacy Officer, at the address below for our free "Will to Survive" legacy advice leaflet.

Please leave something in your will for hunted animals or they'll be left to suffer this cruelty for generations to come.

LEAGUE AGAINST CRUEL SPORTS
WORKING FOR WILDLIFE

League Against Cruel Sports, Sparling House, 83/87 Union Street, London, SE1 1SG 020 7403 6155

DON'T LET BRITAIN'S WILDLIFE GO TO THE DOGS.

Help us transform lives...

Darren was born with Muscular Dystrophy, and at the age of seven life seemed a hopeless ordeal as he struggled to cope in a mainstream school full of able-bodied pupils.

When at last he was referred to a Shaftesbury school with spe-cialist facilities and professional carers who understood his needs, Darren began to thrive. He is now a happy, confident student expecting to gain good qualifications and fulfil his hopes of a successful career.

Darren's life was completely turned around by the care he received from Shaftesbury – but to continue and develop our work we depend heavily on the generosity of our supporters.

Please leave a gift in your will to Shaftesbury so that Darren and others can have lasting hope in the future. See the feature opposite to find out more about our work, or please telephone our Legacy Officer on 0208 239 5555 ext 572.

(Photograph posed by model and name changed to protect confidentiality)

...by making a gift in your will

Shaftesbury
Christian care in action

Registered Charity No 221948
Registered in England No 38751

The Shaftesbury Society –
giving life new meaning

The Shaftesbury Society is one of the country's leading Christian caring charities – supporting people with a disability and those on low incomes, helping them find security, self-worth and significance

Shaftesbury began life over 150 years ago as The Ragged School Union, founded in 1844 under the influence of the Victorian social reformer the 7th Earl of Shaftesbury. He successfully campaigned for changes to many laws that still affect our lives, including those preventing women and children working long hours in factories and mines. The first Ragged Schools were run for the children of families who were too poor to afford proper clothes, let alone an education.

Today, Shaftesbury is one of the country's leading Christian caring charities – providing a range of care and education services for people with disabilities. We provide residential and community-based services for adults; and we run special schools, colleges and initiatives to support families whose children have special needs.

Our other community-based projects work with people on low incomes, tackling needs such as unemployment, homelessness, elder isolation and community regeneration.

We do this from a wide base of contractual and partnership relationships across the country – with local authorities, churches and community groups. In many practical ways, Shaftesbury is working to help individuals reach their full potential, make their own choices and live as valued members of their own communities.

We rely heavily on gifts and will donations to finance our work. For more information about ways of supporting Shaftesbury or any aspect of our work, please contact us at the address below.

The Shaftesbury Society
16 Kingston Road, London SW19 1 JZ
Tel 0208 239 5555
Fax 0208 239 5580

Registered Charity No 221948   Registered in England No 38751

Payment provision for professionals handling probate matters needs to be made in your will as it is highly unlikely that work will be done for free. However, elderly readers should beware of solicitors who include or suggest in any way whatsoever a bequest made to them. Law Society rules contained in the 'Guide to the Professional Conduct of Solicitors', eighth edition (pages 318–19, 4 notes), makes it clear what is acceptable and what is not. If you feel you are being pressured, then change your solicitor, write a codicil removing him/her as an executor and deleting any bequest and, finally, if you feel up to it, report the firm to the Office of Supervision of Solicitors (see below). It would be very interesting to learn from readers if they have come across this problem.

As a co-executor and/or beneficiary, should you feel a solicitor's charge is too high or the work carried out is unsatisfactory, then you can contact the Law Society's Complaints Bureau in writing, explaining the circumstances and asking for its opinion. (Office for the Supervision of Solicitors, Victoria Court, 8 Dormer Place, Leamington Spa, Warwickshire CV32 5AE.) It is worth noting that presently the Law Society is one of the few professional bodies which actively adjudicates for fairness between the public and its members, but it does take persistence and time on your part. Whether the Law Society can effectively 'ride two horses' at the same time is open to debate.

Banks will also advise on preparing wills and dealing with probate matters but at present they have to use a solicitor's services. The fee route is similar to that of solicitors; however, in most instances, banks are more expensive and can take far longer in dealing with your affairs. A proposal in the form of the Courts and Legal Services Act is still awaiting ratification. Once this has been done, a bank will be able to apply direct to the Authority rather than via the services of a solicitor.

Once a will has been made it is no use placing it in an obscure location. You should inform your executor(s) where it will be kept. Indeed, it may be prudent to leave a copy of it with your solicitor or at your bank.

If you die without leaving a will, then the laws of intestacy apply to your estate. This means that your estate is divided among your surviving blood relatives according to specific rules laid down by Parliament. If there are no living relatives, once an extensive search has been undertaken, your money goes to the Crown. This surely must be reason enough for ensuring that you make out a will!

These intestacy rules are, of course, made in broad terms and cannot take account of your individual wishes. So it is possible that a close relative who you may not have wanted to be a beneficiary will take a share of your estate. Conversely, a close friend or relative by marriage whom you may wish to benefit will not do so unless you make a will.

In December 1993 the White Paper's recommendations regarding the financial position of the surviving spouse under intestacy rules were finally passed. This now means that the amount of the surviving spouse's statutory legacy increases from £75,000 to £125,000 if there are children. If there are no children it increases to £200,000, assuming, of course, that the estate has that value in it.

In October 1995 the government passed a new measure called the Law Reform (Succession) Act 1995 which came into effect on 1 January 1996. It amended the 1975 Inheritance Act. By this amendment, it means that the vast majority of couples living outside wedlock can now seek financial provision from the estate of the deceased co-habitee, while at the same time it is understood to leave open the claims from a separated wife and dependent children from any previous marriage.

However, it must be stressed that the Act doesn't automatically give a common-law partner inheritance tax rights on intestacy, merely it seeks to *clarify* the standing of such partners in respect of claims made under the Inheritance (Provision for Family and Dependants) Act 1975. Section 1 of the 1995 Act rules that on intestacy or partial intestacy, a spouse will benefit in the estate provided he or she survives for 28 days after the date of death of the deceased. A spouse who survives for a short time but dies within the 28-day period will be treated as if he or she had died within the lifetime of the deceased.

The second part of the book deals with probate, what steps should be taken and when, in order to prove a will.

If the sad task of winding up the estate of a close relative or friend is placed under your agreed control, you may need to seek advice. The best place to start is at the Personal Applications Department of your nearest Probate Registry or at one of its subregistries. The Registrar and his colleagues in the Personal Applications Department deal on a daily basis with all sorts of queries raised regarding probate. However, they cannot give advice. Of course, the State has laid down certain rules which have to be followed by them. The rules are there to protect the wishes of the deceased and to ensure that those wishes are fulfilled.

Wills can be turned down as invalid but most are accepted as having been properly made according to the laws applicable. The Registrar has some discretion in respect of what may be accepted without query but also has rules to follow. He or she cannot, of course, change a will nor give an opinion as to its meaning other than for the specific purpose of deciding who may be entitled to be appointed to administer the estate.

If your affairs are complicated or involved, this book is not for you. Unless you have the right legal training (or knowledge) you may have to call upon your professional legal adviser in at least one aspect. But the fact that your estate is of considerable value does not in itself create problems except, of course, in inheritance tax planning. The legal procedure to follow is the same whether an estate has little value or great value.

If tax planning is needed, then do seek assistance from a tax consultant.

In probably 95 per cent of cases a layperson is capable of dealing with his or her own affairs without any assistance from professionals. For this majority who feel capable and confident and able to cope within constraints this book is here as a guide.

Finally, it is possible to change the terms of a deceased's will through a document called a Deed of Family Arrangement provided all the beneficiaries agree to the change(s) and are over 18 years of age. It also has to be done within two years from the date of death. Importantly, the Revenue have to agree these changes.

1

Why Do You Need a Will?

For most people the thought of making a will is depressing, confirming the inevitability of our fate, and because of this it is often put aside for another day. Granted such a gloomy task is hardly inspiring. However, sooner or later the task has to be done as it is an essential part of administering your personal affairs.

Most people own their own car, have household furniture, bank and/or building society accounts and a growing number own a house, and some own shares. By making a will you are directing who should receive your possessions following your death. Without one you are considered to have died *intestate* and the intestacy laws apply. In Scottish and English law if there are no traceable surviving relatives then all of your possessions, in other words 'your estate', less any debts or liabilities, go to the Crown.

The greater percentage of the population at present do not bother to make a will. How many times have you said: 'I do not have that much to leave, so why bother to make out a will?' Or, 'There is only this house and my car, so it is not necessary.' Or, 'Why should it concern me who will get what? I will, after all, not be around.' Or, lastly, 'Estate planning? I won't have to pay the tax.'

The wealth of this nation has dramatically increased over the past 15 years. It is not just the privileged few who have money and assets to leave to their family and friends. The increase in house prices was one of the most significant adjustments to personal wealth in the 1980s; in increasing numbers the second generation are inheriting a property in addition to owning their own. And they may own yet another property, which is rented out. Indeed a study by merchant bankers Morgan Grenfell showed that the annual number of inherited properties rose in the last decade by one-third to 128,000. The value of inherited property quadrupled to £8.5 billion with the long-term forecast showing that this will rise even further in the next two decades as 21 million people (86 per cent of them pensioners) will be home owners. The predicted windfalls are estimated to total £35 billion a year!

When you add to this value even modest savings, insurance policies, pensions and so on you can easily see how the inheritance tax threshold of £234,000 means that 1 in 45 persons will be affected. (Remember inheritance from your deceased spouse has no inheritance tax.) Therefore, despite this increase, it does not mean that estate planning can be forgotten. For example, should a married couple hold an estate jointly and its value is over £234,000, then unless they take precautions, the *surviving* person's estate on their death may attract inheritance tax at the current rate.

Inheritance tax is generally regarded as a tax on middle England as the wealthy take great care to provide for continuity of wealth in future generations. The middle classes are more reluctant to prepare for this tax, considering the expense in their lifetime, with the end result that most of the contributions to this tax came from the middle classes.

For those of you undecided on estate planning, it is worth recalling the new Chancellor's words when he was Shadow Chancellor. When his predecessor announced in his Autumn Statement in 1995 that Inheritance Tax was due to be increased to £200,000, Mr Brown stated his disappointment at this action. Yet in the Chancellor's budget on 21 March 2000 Inheritance Tax was increased from £231,000 to £234,000, which increased the number of estates liable to the tax from 21,000 in tax year 1999/00 to 23,500 in 2000/01.

For those readers who are collectors of works of art the Inland Revenue have produced a conditionally exempt works of art register. Conditional exemption from inheritance tax may be granted for works of art and other objects, such as pictures,

Cancer Prevention Research Trust

Purpose and Programme
- To carry out biochemical research into the prevention of cancer.
- To provide funds for research to combat cancer and the human suffering it causes.
- To help sustain critical research programmes.

Broad Objectives
- Develop the means to reduce the effectiveness of environmental agents (carcinogenic chemicals, viruses, radiations) for producing cancer.
- Develop the means to educate the public (e.g. that restriction of intake of calories reduces tumour incidence) in order to minimise cancer development.
- Develop the means to prevent the transformation of normal cells to cells capable of forming cancer.
- Develop means to prevent and control the progression of precancerous cells, (polyps and other innocent tumours) to cancers, the development of cancer from precancerous conditions and the spread of cancers from primary sites.
- Develop the means to achieve an accurate assessment of risk of developing cancer in individuals and in population groups as well as the presence, extent and probable cause of existing cancers.
- Develop the means to treat cancer patients and to control the progress of cancers.
- Develop the means to improve the rehabilitation of cancer patients.

Cancer is a preventable disease

Cancer Prevention Research Trust, Cobden House, 231 Roehampton Lane, London SW15 4LB
Tel: (020) 8785 7786 Fax: (020) 8785 6466
For donations, in memoriam gifts, legacies
Registered Charity No. 265985

Cancer Prevention Research Trust

Cobden House, 231 Roehampton Lane, London SW15 4LB
Tel: (020) 8785 7786 Fax: (020) 8785 6466
RCN: 265985

RESPONDING TO THE CHALLENGE
OF THE CLIMATE OF CHANGE

Our generation's challenge is addressing the very serious problem of increasing cancer deaths.
Unless we act now the future will be bleak.
It is just possible that for many of the forms of cancer the most logical approach will be to find means of prevention.
Most of us have been brought up on a cure-orientated climate. It is time to respond to the challenge of the climate of change, a challenge that demands a serious response from industry and the public.
That is why the Cancer Prevention Research Trust is doing its part in launching this unique initiative.

Preventing cancer is a serious business . . . for all of us.
Cancer is a preventable disease

ITDG PRACTICAL ANSWERS TO POVERTY

ITDG –'Practical Answers To Poverty works with Third World communities on small-scale, self-help projects, building on existing skills and developing new ones.

You can help too, with a donation or legacy. For more information and a free guide to making a Will phone or write to:

Mary Harwood

ITDG, Room 00NA01, The Schumacher Centre for Technology and Development, Bourton Hall, Bourton-on-Dunsmore, Rugby, Warwickshire CV23 9QZ UK
Tel: (01788) 661100

Patron HRH Prince of Wales. Company Reg. No. 871954 Reg. Charity 247257

"When ITDG's people came, we thought they could not help us because they did not bring tools or give us money. But they have helped us much more . . . They have given us the power to make tools ourselves."

Mr. Zinyongo, carpenter

ITDG is a charity founded in 1965 by Dr. Fritz Schumacher, author of Small is Beautiful. "Find out what people are doing," said Schumacher, "and help them do it better."

ITDG's focus is on long term development rather than short term relief. By adding technical expertise and training to people's traditional skills and experience, and encouraging the best use of local resources, ITDG helps communities to work their way out of poverty and improve their quality of life.

ITDG's many projects include improved stoves in Kenya, which can be made by local potters, use less fuelwood and reduce health hazards; earthquake resistant building techniques in Peru; and ways to counter the effects of drought in Zimbabwe.

A donation or legacy to ITDG is a sound investment in the future of the global family.

prints, books, manuscripts and scientific collections which are of national, scientific, historic or artistic interest. The rules for this conditional exemption are that the owner must keep the object in the United Kingdom and allow reasonable public access to the object. Readers can gain further details by purchasing booklet IR67 entitled 'Capital Taxation and the National Heritage' from Public Enquiry Room, First Avenue House, 42–49 High Holborn, London WC1V 2NP (tel: 020 7936 7000).

A growing number of couples now choose to live together outside marriage. This figure is estimated to be one million. Many items, such as the house, are bought jointly. However, until the Law Reform (Succession) Act 1995, which came into effect on 1 January 1996, it meant that the surviving co-habitee did not receive any portion of the deceased's estate *unless* provision had been made in the will. Under this new Bill, the surviving co-habitee can claim financial provision from the deceased's estate.

Problems can occur when writing your own will. The most frequent problem with DIY wills is that they are not worded clearly. Other errors can occur. For example, in Scotland a will, apart from the signatures of the witnesses, must also include the witnesses' full details such as names, addresses and occupations. Again, in Scotland, if the will is handwritten by the testator, ie a holograph will, witnesses are not required.

A will does not come into effect until death has occurred. A testator does not become a testator until he or she dies, nor does an executor become an executor until this happens. So until this event the contents of a will and a will itself can be changed. If there are minor alterations, these changes can be inserted in the form of a codicil. If changes occur frequently or if they are major ones, it is better to write a new will. Remember, if a new will is drawn up, the old one must be destroyed, provided, of course, that you are satisfied that the new one has been drawn up properly and signed and witnessed correctly with the important statement at its beginning (see page 59, clause C), 'I hereby revoke all former wills codicils and testamentary provisions at any time made by me and declare this to be my last will'.

You can also include in your will any specific arrangements you may wish to make regarding your own funeral. Or perhaps you may wish to donate your body to medical research or organ donation. So a will is used not only for listing who should receive what asset from your estate but also for any other wishes you may have. Your executor should also be made aware of certain provisions in your will, namely funeral arrangements. Your wish with regard to organ donations needs to be known by those closest to you in order to fulfil your wishes.

If there is a rule when writing your own will it must be to keep it simple. Do not stray into legal technicalities. Instead, set out what gifts are to be made, clearly identifying all objects and stating who should receive them.

Since 1964, even if you hold a foreign passport but are still permanently resident in this country, there is no distinction in law between owning property in the United Kingdom (under English law) and leaving it in your will to a person who resides abroad. Property can also be held overseas and left to someone residing in this country.

Distribution of immovable property held overseas has to be carried out in accordance with the law of the land in which that property is situated. This should serve as a reminder, when purchasing property overseas, to enquire what inheritance tax laws apply there. Legal advice in such cases should always be sought.

Who can make a will?

1. A child under the age of 18 cannot generally make a will.

However, if you are under the age of 18 and in Her Majesty's armed forces on active service, then you will be able to make a will which will stand as a valid one.

2. A person of sound mind.

Obviously a person must be of sound mind and capable of managing his or her affairs when signing a will. However, if after making your will, through illness or an accident, you become unsound of mind the will remains valid.

The point at which a person becomes unsound of mind can be challenged and so, if challenging, it is important to be able to substantiate the condition medically.

The Mental Health Act defines a person suffering from severe subnormality as one who is in a state 'of incomplete development of mind which includes sub-normality of intelligence and is of such a nature or degree that the patient is incapable of living an independent life or of guarding himself against serious exploitation or will be so incapable of an age to do so.'

Great Uncle Herbert talking to himself in the garden or your grandmother having an invisible friend is not cause for challenging either will in court. In all probability they would not be seen as being of unsound mind but possibly suffering from a mild dose of eccentricity.

Decide on your aims

Before making a will think what you want to achieve by it. Are you married? Have you any children? Are there any other beneficiaries you wish to include, such as parents, brothers, sisters, distant relatives? Are you likely to leave any money to charity? Have you considered organ donation?

Once you have considered what you want to achieve then draw up a list noting exactly what assets you have and how best to distribute your estate to fulfil your wishes. Whatever you own is considered to be an *asset*: a car, any items of furniture, jewellery, paintings, house, securities and so on. Add to this any money you may have in savings accounts, along with details of any insurance policies or investments you hold. Literally, everything you own should be listed, from half-shares in the family silver to half-shares in an old jalopy.

Now list, in order of priority, those people you wish to benefit from your will. You may want your daughter to have all your jewellery and a friend might appreciate a specific item such as a ring, a painting or any item that holds particular fond memories. If you are a parent, you will probably wish your children to receive the money from your life insurance policy, a share of the house, any pension rights you have, investments and so on. Alternatively, you may decide to split it, leaving some to your spouse and the rest to your children. You might want your church or favourite charities to receive a sum of money. Whatever you decide, note alongside each item whom you wish it to go to.

A will is the 'last wish' of a person and so expresses what you want to happen after your death. However, some wishes may

not be actionable. For example, if you do not ask the people who you have selected to be your executors whether they are prepared to take on the task, they could well turn it down. You may wish to be buried in your local churchyard, but without prior permission from the vicar you may be put to rest in another cemetery. And if you died while living abroad but wished to be buried in this country, arrangements would have to be made (and finance found) to bring your body back.

Again, another example is that of guardianship. If you wish to appoint a person or persons as your children's guardians in the case of your and your spouse's death, then do ensure that you have their agreement that they are willing to take on this responsibility. Also, you will need to have a special document drawn up by your solicitor.

How much will my estate be worth in, say, 20 years' time?

How long is a piece of string? This eventuality is, however, taken care of. Your executor values your estate at the date of death.

Any items not specially mentioned in your will would come under the term 'residue of estate', in other words everything you own or have legal title to. Whoever is left the residue of the estate would inherit the additional items not already disposed of. But, to ensure that a newly acquired specific gift goes to the right person, as your personal circumstances change so should your will. Every few years examine your present situation and, if necessary, make out a new will. If there are only minor amendments, then a codicil can be drawn up.

Understanding the jargon

So far in this text fairly straightforward words have been used, such as estate, beneficiary, testator, residue and so on. However, there are some less familiar words that you will come across and which will be used quite frequently from now on. The next few pages contain a glossary of terms of such words and phrases.

protecting wildlife for the next generation

Protecting our countryside and our environment is one of the most important issues facing us today, whoever we are, wherever we live. The wildlife and wild places of Yorkshire are probably the most varied of any in Britain, and with over 70 nature reserves the Yorkshire Wildlife Trust, manages, promotes and protects, plants, animals and their habitats throughout the whole county. As urban sprawl encroaches, life will be poorer without the wild flowers and creatures, the woods and moors, fields and rivers, the Yorkshire Wildlife Trust strives to protect for this generation and the next. Wherever you're from, but especially if Yorkshire is or was home to you, a legacy or donation to the Trust will help it achieve its aim which is:

To conserve and promote the diversity of Yorkshire wildlife and habitat for the benefit and well being of both wildlife and people.

For further information contact:
Stephen B Suart, Yorkshire Wildlife Trust Development Office,
Beech house, Thormandy, York YO61 4NN   Phone/Fax: 01845-501000

Yorkshire Wildlife Trust Ltd, Registered in England as a Company Ltd by Guarantee No. 409650
Registered Office: 10 Toft Green, York YO61 4NN   Registered Charity No. 210807.   Vat No. 170 391475.

Yorkshire Wildlife Trust 10 Toft Green, York YO61 4NN. (Tel: (01904) 659570)

The Trust is the County Nature Conservation Trust for Yorkshire; it was founded in 1946 to purchase its first nature reserve, Askham Bog near York. It is a registered charity (No. 210807), Its aim is to promote the diversity of Yorkshire Wildlife and habitats for the benefits and well being of both wildlife and people by acquiring and managing sites of national, regional and local significance in the County and by encouraging local landowners to include conservation as a criterion in the management of their holdings. It seeks to ensure a good distribution of nature reserves throughout the County to ensure that the region's characteristic habitats, geographic structure and topography are represented.

The Trust now has over 7000 members and 80 reserves. Its 80 reserves are open at all times unless it is necessary to restrict access temporarily to permit the breeding and rearing of young or to protect rare plants during the flowering season. The Trust's nature reserves and management sites are scattered across the length and breath of the County, some in very remote areas, others adjacent to a or partially enclosed by large urban areas; the total acreage is approximately 8,000.

Pressures from both agriculture and industry since the Trust was incorporated in 1946 have changed the face of the countryside dramatically and in conservation terms, for the worse. In the last ten years this pressure has, if anything, become more intense, and there is now an increasing awareness amongst the general public and industry of the need to protect the countryside and the remaining habitat it contains. The Trust is involved in planning and development proposals where wildlife is affected.

Its nature reserves, while providing protection for all forms of wildlife, also provide the public with many benefits, they allow people to develop a greater awareness and appreciation of the countryside which helps to improve the richness and quality of their lives.

The Trust regards education, in the broadest meaning of the word, as a cornerstone of its policy. Its nature reserves are used by schools to introduce school children to nature and ecological studies and to develop their understanding of conservation principles and management. Several of them are also used by universities and colleges for research work.

A LEGACY TO THE MUSICIANS BENEVOLENT
FUND CAN DO SO MUCH TO HELP NEEDY
MUSICIANS AND THOSE IN CLOSELY
RELATED OCCUPATIONS - FOR WHOM
ACCIDENT OR ILLNESS CAN LEAD TO
DESPAIR AND EVEN SILENCE.
PLEASE SEND US A DONATION AND CONSIDER
REMEMBERING US IN YOUR WILL.

MUSICIANS
BENEVOLENT FUND

SILENCE?

MUSICIANS BENEVOLENT FUND, 16 OGLE STREET, LONDON W1P 8JB
TEL: 020 7636 4481 FAX: 020 7637 4307
EMAIL: info@mbf.org.uk WEBSITE: http://www.mbf.org.uk
REGISTERED CHARITY No.228089

Musicians Benevolent Fund

Professional musicians can often face stress and uncertainty. When accident and illness strike, life can become a nightmare. The Musicians Benevolent Fund spends around £1 million helping about 1,000 musicians and people who work, or have worked, in occupations closely related to music each year. Each case is treated individually and in the strictest of confidence.

The MBF will do all in its power to get a musician back to work, where this is not possible it can help in a number of ways. Trained visitors call on beneficiaries in their own homes, assessing their needs and offering practical help and advice including arranging for long and short term care; counselling; financial support; mobility aids and instrument adaptation. Ivor Newton House, the MBF's residential home in Bromley, Kent offers relaxed and comfortable surroundings for musicians and music lovers alike.

Younger musicians and those at the start of their professional careers can be helped through the MBF's Education Awards and other award schemes. Over 20 award schemes are administered by the MBF and cover a broad range of ages up to age 30. The annually published Handbook of Music Awards and Scholarships lists the MBF awards and many others, with useful advice and tips for students.

The MBF relies on legacies and donations to continue this essential work. Leaflets about the Fund's work and their legacy leaflet 'The Final Round of Applause' are available from the Secretary at the address below or you may wish to telephone to arrange a personal and confidential meeting to discuss your wishes.

Musicians Benevolent Fund
16 Ogle Street
London
W1P 8JB
Tel: 020 7636 4481
Fax: 020 7637 4307
e-mail: info@mbf.org.uk
Website: www.mbf.org.uk
Secretary: Helen Faulkner
Head of Casework: Sara Dixon
RCN: 228089

Absolute. Given without any condition. For example, 'I give to… the residue of my estate absolutely' means just that. Whatever is left in the estate is given absolutely over to that named person.

Administrator. A person appointed by the Probate Registry in the absence of a will being found or a person who is appointed to prove a will in the event of there being no executor. A relative or close friend of a beneficiary could be asked to administer the estate in order of beneficial priority.

Assets. Your possessions which, apart from bank accounts, insurance policies etc, include furniture, cars, jewellery – generally everything.

Beneficiary. A person who inherits (benefits) under a will or under intestacy laws or under a trust.

Bequest. A gift of estate (other than immovable property such as houses or land).

Bond of caution. According to Scottish law it represents a sum of money which can compensate the estate for any loss caused by an executor's mistake or omission.

Chargeable gift. An item given under the conditions of a will on which tax may have to be paid.

Children. This term now covers both legitimate and illegitimate children, also children who have been legally adopted into the family. It does not include stepchildren. Such persons must therefore be specifically mentioned if they are to benefit under a will. Children who are born as a result of a sperm bank donation have to be specifically named in the will. Mentioning their existence or possible existence without specific title, albeit that instructions are given in the will, could lead to that wish not being fulfilled. At this point, because of the newness of sperm bank donation, this issue is considered to be dangerous, uncharted legal ground and specialist legal advice should be sought.

Codicil. A formal legal document which can be used to make small changes to your will later on.

Confirmation. The Scottish equivalent of a grant of probate.

Crown. This refers to the Government, whatever department.

Deceased. The person who has died.

Descendants. Any member of your blood line, such as children, grandchildren and so on.

Devise and bequeath. To give a gift under a will or codicil.

Distribution. The process of dealing with an estate after receiving the Grant of Probate or Letters of Administration, first paying debts and then dividing up the remainder between the beneficiaries.

Docket. Scottish term for a formal note.

Donee. A person who receives a gift.

Donor. A person who gives a gift.

Engrossment. Final copy of a legal document.

Excepted estates. This is where an estate gains exemption to supply accounts to the Inland Revenue provided certain strict criteria are met, in particular where the value of the estate does not exceed £200,000, and consists of property passed under a will or intestacy or nomination or by survivorship. No more than £50,000 of its value should consist of property outside the United Kingdom and the deceased must have died domiciled in the United Kingdom, having made no lifetime gifts chargeable to either inheritance tax or capital transfer tax or life interests into settlement. In the case of excepted estates, a Grant of Representation can be applied for to the Inland Revenue where applicants have already gained probate or letters of administration.

Executor. A person appointed by you in your will to deal with the estate. This person cannot charge a fee unless previously authorised by the will, although he or she is able to reclaim out-of-pocket expenses.

Husband. Your spouse who is still alive at the time the will is made (the same definition for Wife). In the case of divorce under English law, a couple are still legally married until the decree absolute. For Scottish law, see Chapter 11.

Infant. Now usually referred to as a Minor, in other words a person who is under the age of 18. The law at the moment states that a minor cannot legally hold possessions from an estate until the age of 18. If an asset has been given, then it is given under the terms of a trust to the parent or guardian (known as a trustee) for the benefit of the infant until the age of majority has been reached. You can, if you wish, declare that the minor is to take possession of the legacy before he or she attains his or her age of majority for a specific purpose.

Interest. The right to your property. If total, then it is called *Absolute Interest*.

Intestate. Dying without a will; the rules of intestacy apply, see Chapter 2.

Issue. This means all living descendants.

Joint tenant. This term is applied when two or more people jointly own property. Upon the death of one of them that person's share passes to the surviving joint tenant or tenants. However, the value of the estate that is passed on to the surviving tenant(s) still has to be calculated for inheritance tax purposes. No tax is payable if the surviving joint tenant is the spouse.

Legacy. A gift of money or property other than house or land.

Legal rights. Under Scottish law this means that the surviving spouse and/or children are entitled, irrespective of the will, to benefit from the estate. Limited rights for a spouse are also now included in English law.

Life interest. The right to enjoy the benefit for life of either money or house or land or, in fact, any property. It reverts to

the testator's estate upon the death of the person who enjoyed the life interest.

Life tenant. The person who benefits from a life interest.

Moveable property. This refers to any property other than land or buildings.

Next of kin. Your closest living relative.

Pecuniary legacy. A specific gift of money in your will, eg 'I give £100 to John Brown'.

Personal representative. The person appointed by the Probate Court to deal with your estate in a Grant of Representation. (This would include an executor named by you in your will.)

Power of appointment. The right to nominate persons to receive the benefit of a trust after your death. (Usually the person given the power is the present life tenant of the trust.)

Probate. The document issued by the Probate Court which pronounces the validity of a will and upholds the appointment of executor. In Scotland this document is known as *Confirmation*.

Residue. The remainder of an estate after all legacies and bequests have been given to the donees and once all debts, taxes and expenses have been paid.

Small estate. In Scotland it means an estate where the gross value is less than £25,000. This should not be confused with those estates in England and Wales where, because of the small amounts of money involved, ie under £5,000 and termed 'small estates', it is possible to obtain release of the monies in the estate without the legal formality of applying for a Grant.

Survivor. Any relative mentioned in the will who is still alive at the time of the testator's death. It also applies to those who may not have been born at the time the will was made but are referred to in it, subject to limitations.

Tenant-in-common. An alternative to joint tenancy for two or more persons to hold property. In this manner each has a separate share which forms part of his or her estate on death and does not automatically pass to the surviving tenant(s) in common but will pass either under the will or on intestacy.

Testamentary expenses. The cost of administering a will, eg expenses such as telephone, stamps, loss of wages and so on.

Testator. A person who makes a will.

Trust. Parts of an estate (or a whole estate) administered by trustees for the benefit of a named person in accordance with the trust document.

Trustee. A person nominated to deal with a trust.

2

What Happens If You Die Without a Valid Will?

If you die without leaving a valid will, you are said to have died *intestate*. Usually in instances where one spouse dies before the other, depending on the estate's size, all or the greatest share of the estate goes to the surviving spouse.

The present intestacy laws date back to 1858 when Probate Registries were first introduced. Since then they have been regularly updated to try to take account of the changes in personal circumstances and the change in the value of money.

The intestacy law, however, was considered by some to need a complete review. The general opinion was that this law no longer adequately met the needs for distributing the average person's estate and has subsequently been altered. Now if there is a surviving spouse and issue, then the spouse receives a lump sum, known as the *statutory legacy* and half of the remaining estate for his or her life. *Life interest* means that the spouse cannot spend the capital of the life interest and may only use the interest obtained from investing that sum. The statutory legacy has been increased to £125,000 if the deceased leaves issue. The value increases to £200,000 if there are no children, provided that the estate has that amount of value in it.

Present rules

As the intestacy law stands, if a person dies without a will and leaves a child or other issue, then such person(s) will benefit from the realisation of all investments, property, etc on reaching the age of 18. If he or she is not 18, then the share is held in trust until the child reaches the age of majority, when usually he or she is able to receive it. However, the trustees may, in certain circumstances, advance monies from the trust for the purpose of 'maintenance, education or advancement of the child'. When the child eventually receives the trust's estate it should include any interest earned on the money.

It cannot be stressed too often that the prime importance of making a will is that you are able to specify whom you wish to deal with your affairs and to whom you wish to leave your estate. If you do not make a will and you die leaving no traceable relatives, your estate will go to the Crown and will form part of government funds. By making a will and appointing an executor, one of the advantages is the flexibility allowed to that executor to move money around in a variable market in order to make the safest investment for your appointed heirs.

If an executor has not been appointed in a will, or if a will has not been made out, then the deceased's property, including personal belongings, will be administered by a personal representative. This representative is appointed by the Probate

This is a typical North African foal. Taken from her mother and put to work as soon as her legs can take it, she will be underfed and worked until she is fit to drop. She will get ill; no one will help and she will die in agony. Only then will she be free from her torment.

Will you remember me?

To help foals like her, SPANA needs people like you to remember… Please include a bequest for the donkeys in your will

Send for SPANA's FREE information

SPANA
PROTECTS ANIMALS ABROAD

SPANA's trained dressers provide treatment for suffering animals and a massive education campaign is teaching people to care for animals properly.

SPANA, Dept HWWGP, FREEPOST (SW 6038), London SW1E 6YY

Registry in accordance with strict rules of priority. These rules state that a spouse has the first right to be appointed to administer the deceased's estate. But if the surviving spouse does not feel willing or able to handle the job, the couple's children may be appointed to act on their parent's behalf. When there is no surviving spouse or children then the task of administering the estate can fall on close relatives, ie parents, brothers, sisters or their issue. A close friend may be appointed attorney of the person entitled to act and, if suitable, will be appointed administrator, although this does not often happen.

Whoever is appointed has a duty to administer the estate to see that, where necessary, the assets are sold at the best possible price and any debts and expenses paid off. Once that has been done, distribution takes place in accordance with the Administration of Estates Act. This Act governs the distribution of an estate when the deceased has died intestate. Under the Act, if you were the appointed representative, you would have the power to deal with the estate as you thought fit in order to safeguard the assets. Of course, you are accountable for your actions.

You can claim administrative costs and out-of-pocket expenses from the estate, such as stamps, telephone calls and so on. Also, if you have had to forfeit a day's pay in attending to estate affairs you can reclaim the amount of pay lost.

After *letters of administration* have been granted by the Probate Registry and once all debts and expenses have been paid distribution can take place. Again, there is an order of priority.

If there is a surviving spouse *and* issue, the spouse receives all the deceased's personal items (known as *personal effects*) together with a sum up to the value of the statutory legacy which is £125,000. Should the value of the estate exceed this and there is also issue, then the surviving spouse would receive half of the balance of the estate for life. In other words, the half of what remains after the personal effects, the statutory legacy of £125,000, and debts and expenses have been deducted. The remaining half would go to any children immediately, except if they are under the age of 18 (see page 23). If any child did die in the lifetime of the deceased leaving children of his or her own, then those children would divide their parent's share between them.

On the death of the surviving spouse the half of the estate which he or she has had a life interest in would pass to the children. Therefore, it is important to understand fully what *life interest* means. Life interest could be described as borrowed ownership in that you have the right to use the interest from the capital but cannot touch the capital as it does not legally belong to you. Upon death, the life interest passes to the other beneficiaries, for example, the children, and is divided up equally for their benefit. Again, if any children of the deceased died in his or her lifetime leaving children of their own, then the same applies as in the above paragraph.

When children are the nearest surviving relatives of the deceased, the estate passes to them or, if some have already died leaving children of their own, to their issue, ie grandchildren or great grandchildren of the testator. The shares are held in a *statutory trust* for the children, in equal parts, until each reaches the age of 18 or marries, whichever happens first. The definition of children now includes legitimate, illegitimate or legally adopted children but not stepchildren (see page 22).

In a case where there is a surviving spouse but *no* issue, the spouse's statutory legacy increases to £200,000 in addition to the personal effects. If the estate is larger than this and there are no surviving issue, but other relations are alive, such as parents, brothers, sisters, etc, then the spouse receives all the personal effects together with £200,000 and half of the residue of the estate absolutely, with no life interest being applicable.

If a brother or sister of the deceased dies in the deceased's lifetime, leaving children, then their children will take the deceased parent's share divided equally between them.

Should a person die leaving a surviving spouse but no children, or other issue, or indeed parents, brothers or sisters or their issue, in other words no blood relative, the surviving spouse receives the whole of the estate, irrespective of its value.

The order of inheritance of an estate where the deceased has died intestate is as follows:

1. spouse;
2. children or their issue;
3. parents;

4. brothers and sisters of the 'whole blood' or, if deceased, their issue (such issue will divide their deceased parent's share between them);
5. brothers and sisters of the 'half blood' (having one common parent with the deceased) or, if deceased, their issue;
6. grandparents;
7. uncles and aunts of the 'whole blood' or, if deceased, their issue;
8. uncles and aunts of the 'half blood' or, if deceased, their issue;
9. and if there are none of the above, then the estate goes to the Crown.

Often you will see a notice in the national or local papers asking for the relatives of the deceased to contact a firm of solicitors. This usually means that the administrators are trying to trace relatives of the deceased. There is a time stipulation, however. A person cannot turn up some four years after the advertisement to claim his or her inheritance; by then it will be too late, though it is wise for an administrator to take out some form of indemnity cover if there are known beneficiaries who cannot as yet be traced.

Sadly, disputes do arise whether or not you leave a will. However, because of the existence of a will, provided it is properly worded, these disputes can be reduced.

From 1 January 1996, common-law wives receive an income from the deceased partner's estate and property rights, provided they have lived together for two or more years.

In England and Wales if a marriage has ended in divorce and a decree absolute has been granted, the divorced spouse is not entitled to any part of the estate. Their children, however, will be beneficiaries. If death took place after decree nisi had been given but before the granting of decree absolute, then a spouse would still be seen in the eyes of the law to be the surviving spouse and would benefit accordingly. A spouse does not benefit if a judicial separation decree has been issued. A separation order issued by magistrates does not affect entitlement to benefit.

A divorce in England and Wales (for Scotland, see page 138) alters your will and makes any gift to your ex-spouse void.

However, the application of the law that creates this effect on other persons in your will may not operate as you would expect. It is very important, therefore, that a new will be made out when major events alter your life. Remember that once the new will has been written, signed and witnessed, you must destroy the old one.

When a person makes a will and then later marries, in England and Wales, such a will is completely revoked or in some circumstances only revoked in part unless it states that it is being made 'in contemplation of' that forthcoming marriage, and importantly also states that the will is to remain in force after that marriage. If you are considering making a will before an anticipated marriage and you wish for the will to continue after your marriage, you would be strongly advised to consult a solicitor for advice.

3

What You Should Know Before Writing a Will

Anything that is fully owned by you can be left in a will. Certain assets, such as those owned under a joint ownership which are already subject to an agreement to be passed on, cannot be given. Also, any property which has been left to a person under a *form of nomination* (in other words National Savings Bank account) is not covered by your will even if it is referred to.

As years pass by the value of most possessions usually increases. A will written 10 or 15 years ago will be outdated as, it is to be hoped, your possessions will have increased substantially both in quantity and value. This is why it is important to update your will by making a new one. You may also be the beneficiary of someone else's will and may wish to name the person who, in turn, is to inherit this gift in your will. Incidentally, provided that you survive the donor, you, and ultimately your beneficiaries, will inherit the gift, assuming you have not disposed of it.

This does not mean rewriting your will every year but assessing every few years whether your existing will still adequately covers all your wishes and, indeed, whether your personal circumstances have changed.

What is termed as 'property'?

Whatever you own from a house to personal effects is your *property*, and forms your *estate*.

In addition, there is a distinction between freehold and leasehold property not only in definition but, more importantly, in the context of this book, in the way it forms part of your estate. Owning the freehold of the land and buildings means it is yours for perpetuity. Leasehold property is only owned by you for the duration of the leasehold tenancy or the remaining life of the lease. Leasehold property usually starts its life on a tenancy of 99 years or, in some unusual instances, 999 years. As time passes, so the lease's term decreases until the expiry date is reached.

So you can in theory leave your leasehold flat or house to your nearest relations. However, if the leasehold agreement states that you cannot assign the lease without consent of the owner of the lease, then your executor would first have to seek his or her permission before selling the property or assigning the lease to your beneficiaries (see pages 143–44). You can, of course, write to the lease owner and ask him to sell the lease of your house to you, but you only have the automatic legal right to purchase if you have lived there for four or more years. For owners of flats, luckily, legislation is in hand to give the flat owner the right to purchase the lease of a flat. Consult your solicitor on this matter if you intend to exercise your right.

Another direction that you can include in your will is with regard to the disposal of your body. You may wish to give particular directions for your funeral or even for what you want to have done with your body. Today it is becoming increasingly popular to carry donor cards which can be obtained at doctors' surgeries or from the National Transplant list based in Bristol. These cards authorise the use of various organs in your body for transplant purposes after your death in order to save lives. The organs are removed shortly after death once the donor card(s) has been passed on to the doctor or subject to your nearest of kin's agreement. The next of kin can also give authorisation for removal of organs once a patient has been pronounced dead. Do ensure that your next of kin is fully aware of this wish to save and promote life after yours has ended, and that they will fulfil this intention.

Financial matters

Insurance policies

There are three main types of insurance policy that will pay out on death. First there is a *life policy*, which, upon proof that death has occurred, ie a death certificate, will pay out the insured amount absolutely.

There is a further type of term insurance called the *family income benefit*. While a standard life insurance would pay out a fixed lump sum upon proof of death, family income benefit, acting as a replacement wage, would pay out each and every year throughout its term. There is an added benefit in that the amount can be made inflation proof.

This policy is not only applicable to men but should be considered by women as well. More and more women are wage earners but a fair proportion still remain at home looking after their children. Should a 'stay at home' mother die, how will the husband afford to hire a live-in nanny to care for their children? The cost of a nanny or home help varies but on average you would pay £5,000 to £10,000 a year, plus National Insurance contributions, depending on qualifications, experience and the involvement and time required.

This is another area that needs in-depth consideration. The stress that the death of a partner brings is bad enough without the added worry of insufficient money to cover the basic bills. The surviving spouse needs time to come to terms with his or her grief and that of their children rather than worrying where the next pound is coming from or having to work all hours to make ends meet. Thinking that parents will step in and help is not a practical alternative as in many cases this is not possible through ill-feelings, poor health or lack of money themselves.

The family income benefit's term is based on the youngest member of the family. So if you have three children ranging in age from 3 to 15, the policy would pay out for 15 years until the youngest child reached the age of 18.

If the policy's period of time is 12 years and you die six months into that term, your family will benefit. There is a minus side: if you die 11 years and six months into a 12-year policy, your family will only receive payment for the remaining portion of time, namely six months. You can hedge your bets, however, by taking out a level-term policy which would pay out the same amount irrespective of whether you died 6 months or 6 years after the policy came into force.

Second, there is the *endowment policy*. Although it is not a life policy, it usually has a life element written in. For example, you take out an endowment policy for a lump sum to be paid to you in, say, 10, 15 or 20 years' time and pay a monthly premium to the insurance company. That policy will, in most cases, have a death clause which says that if death occurs before the policy term has been completed a specifically stated sum of money will be paid out.

Last, there is a *pensions policy*, which again, like the endowment policy, usually contains a death clause paying out during the term of the policy upon death.

To realise money from an insurance policy, you have to produce the death certificate along with the policy documents, and, provided you are the beneficiary of that policy and can prove this, the money will be released. Before sending all these documents off under registered post, do telephone the insurance company's head office asking for their specific requirements, and do remember to keep photocopies of all documents sent.

If you are over 45 you will be able as a widow to claim a widow's pension, which is based upon your spouse's contributions. The amount can be increased if you have children under 18 and still in education. This amount must be included on your tax return as it forms part of your income.

Inheritance tax has to be paid once the threshold has been exceeded and before probate is granted, except of course, where there is a direction that the estate is left to the surviving spouse. Although payment of this tax is due on a house or land or any interest held in a private firm, it can be deferred for up to six months from the end of the month in which death took place. The tax on this part of the estate may also be paid by instalments.

If you feel that either you (if you are the beneficiary of a will) or your close relatives (beneficiaries of your will) will not be able to meet the immediate charge of inheritance tax, you can take out a life policy to cover this provision provided you have an *insurable interest*. For example, a husband can take out this policy on his wife's life or she on his because a husband or his wife has an 'insurable interest', though this would seem to be paying out money for the sake of it if the wife/husband were the sole beneficiary. If you are a single person and your brother, sister or parent was the sole beneficiary of your will, then that person would also be able to take out a policy on your life.

In life insurance, *term insurance* is the cheapest and it is best to shop around to find the best deal for you. Incidentally, the premium paid by women is less as they are considered to live longer.

Whole of life is a more expensive life insurance as it guarantees a lump sum of money without stipulating a qualifying period. It also comes with a bonus option. Again, shop around for the deal best suited to your needs.

If you have life insurance as a means of paying inheritance tax, it is wise to keep abreast of the tax threshold to ensure adequate cover.

Whatever type of life policy you do decide to take out, remember that the interest from this policy's payout may provide the only income for your family's living expenses in your absence. Equate this with the cost of the insurance, and the term or period of time which it covers, and its affordability.

Consider what your financial input currently is and what it is likely to be. Next, consider what your family's current and future requirements are. How old are your children? What school are they currently at and will they be going on to higher education? Do not put the onus on to, say, your parents to provide for their grandchildren in the event of your death. This may not happen and it leaves your spouse with trying to cope financially at a time of extreme stress.

Money

The definition of money in a will is taken to mean all cash held, including your loose cash, whether in a purse or wallet or hidden under the bed. It also extends to a range of cash investment accounts, depending upon the context in which the will is written. These accounts range from National Savings accounts to bank and building society accounts and premium bonds. Gifts of money are termed *pecuniary legacies*.

Shares, unit trusts, Personal Equity Plans (PEPs), Individual Savings Plans (ISAs)

As the investment markets introduce new types of investment products, so these new investments may be bought by you and in turn find their way into your will. Shares, unit trusts and PEPs can be disposed of just as if they were any other type of property given within the scope of your will. Share dividends sent after the owner's death also form part of the estate. It is still early days, but ISAs were introduced on 6 April 1999. In the first year a maximum of £7,000 could be put in and in his budget 2000 address the Chancellor announced the extension of time on that limit to 5 April 2001. See page 125–26 for further details.

These assets will have to be valued as at the date of death. This subject is dealt with in detail in Chapter 10, Valuing and Administering the Estate.

However, if there is a life interest noted in your will, be very careful as to the wording of it in relation to the investment in unit trusts and shares as values can go down as well as up. In addition, the purchase of certain investments can actually produce a capital loss.

What is an executor? Who can be appointed?

An executor is a person who is named by you in your will to see that your wishes are carried out in accordance with the will, collect in the estate, pay any debts or expenses and then distribute the remainder to the named beneficiaries. Executors' duties only commence once death has occurred and these duties cease once the estate has been distributed to the named beneficiaries.

You should always appoint someone to be the executor of your will. Before naming that person in your will it is best to ask him or her if he or she is willing to take on the duty. It is useful but not essential to appoint someone who has had previous business experience. Whoever is appointed, once the appointment is accepted, he or she is obliged to carry out your exact wishes.

You may name as many executors as you wish but only four may be appointed to act by the Probate Registry at any one time. It is useful, though not essential, to name more than one person so that if one decides not to act there will still be someone else already appointed and familiar with your wishes. If only one executor is appointed and then turns down this role, the Probate Registry will apply the various rules and regulations to decide who should act in his or her place.

You can appoint a close friend or relative or a firm of solicitors, accountants or your bank to be the executor of your will. A minor or a person of unsound mind will not be allowed to act. Do be aware that if professionals agree to act, then a fee raised against the estate will, be charged. This fact will have to be written into the will, stating that fees and expenses will be paid by the estate. Unless specified, a non-professional executor cannot charge a fee. There is nothing to prevent an executor from receiving a gift under the provisions laid out in the will but this gift will be seen to have been made on condition that he or she acts as executor, unless you state otherwise.

A private individual who acts as an executor and incurs expenses in carrying out those duties can claim back these expenses from the estate. However, he or she is not allowed to charge for time spent carrying out these duties. If, in an official capacity, an executor takes time off work and as a result loses money, then he or she is able to reclaim it from the estate as administration expenses.

If you have been appointed an executor but feel, for whatever reason, after the death that you cannot act, then you may renounce your executorship. You would be asked to sign a *form of renunciation* either by the Probate Registry or by the solicitor acting for other persons named in the will. Should you be holding the will but for some reason are unable to pass the document on to another interested person, then you may file the will at your nearest Probate Registry, signing a form stating that you do not, for whatever reason, wish to deal with the will. The Probate Registry will then appoint a personal representative, usually the chief beneficiary of the will. The person thus appointed is known as the *administrator*.

Even if a professional has been named as one of your executors, he or she does not have an overriding right over other executors to administer your will. Each executor has the right to hold estate assets and apply for probate, with the agreement of all named executors. Joint applications can be made.

Where should a will be kept?

There is no legal obligation to register a will in any official office. This applies wherever you live in the United Kingdom.

It is up to you to keep your will in a secure place and to inform your executors or your nearest relatives of its location. If it is in a safe at home, then let the executor know the combination. If it is locked in a drawer, then let him or her have a key. Should you choose your solicitor or your bank to be one of the executors they will usually keep the will in their safe for you.

Wills can be deposited for safekeeping with the record keeper at Somerset House. You may do this through your local Probate Registry or by calling at or writing to the Probate Dept, Principal Registry, Family Division, First Avenue House, 42–49 High Holborn, London WC1N 6NP (Tel 020 7936 6983). If you write, a large envelope with instructions will be sent to you. All details asked for have to be noted, and it has to be signed and witnessed before being returned. Once Somerset House is in receipt of your will they will send you a deposit certificate. If you present the will personally they will hand the certificate over at that time. This certificate has to be produced by your executors after your death before the will is released to them.

The fee for keeping a will at Somerset House is nominal. There are obvious advantages of doing it this way in that your executors know where the will is and you can rest assured that it is in one of the safest places. The drawback is that should you wish to add a codicil to your will or make out a new one, you will have to produce the certificate before withdrawing the original will. The whole procedure will have to be gone through once again and a second fee would then be charged.

What is a trust?

It is not within the scope of this book to deal with the setting up of a trust, therefore the next few paragraphs are only a brief description.

If a trust is to be formed, you should ask a solicitor who specialises in probate matters to draw one up. Remember that if a trust or life interest is to be included in a will, the costs to administer it can be expensive.

A trust would have been formed if the deceased felt that the beneficiaries would be better catered for by one; or if the beneficiaries are under the age of majority and their needs both present and future need careful administration; for tax reasons; or because the deceased felt that his or her estate should be passed on in perpetuity.

By creating a trust you place your estate (or part of it) in the hands of a person who is called a *trustee*. This person is appointed to a position of trust to carry out the provisions as expressed in the trust.

Before making the trust, ask the person whether he or she wishes to be a trustee. It is best to select at least two people to become trustees.

Trustees are legally bound to deal with the trust and its assets properly and to ensure that any beneficiary of the trust receives what is rightfully due to them.

As in the case of executorship, a trustee does not receive a specific payment for his or her time unless the trust stipulates to the contrary. Of course, expenses can be reclaimed from the trust. Naturally, professionals, whether they are banks, solicitors or accountants, will charge for their time and so you must be aware of what cost is likely to be incurred before creating the trust document.

There are a few points which you should be aware of if you are setting up a trust.

1. You cannot compel a person to act as a trustee.
2. A full inventory of the trust's property must be made at the outset.
3. If there is a life interest, it should state this fact in the trust and ensure that it gives the trustees power to look after whatever is included in the life interest, whether it is money, property, paintings, etc.
4. The trustees are legally bound to carry out the duty specified in the trust within the laws of the land.
5. Trustees are accountable for any neglect or default throughout the administration of the estate.

There have been instances where life tenants or beneficiaries of the trust have felt that they had been unjustly treated. Policing trusts is difficult and unless it can be proved that those involved in administering the trust have shown malice or that fraud has taken place, there is little that can be done. The role of trustee is a difficult one as the trustee must follow the trust's wishes absolutely but still balance the interests of the life tenant. Should anyone feel that they have been treated unjustly they should take proof of this to a solicitor, who in turn will write to the trustees in the hope of resolving matters.

Small estates in England and Wales

Not to be confused with the definition applied in Scotland (see page 130), in England and Wales estates totalling £5,000 or less are considered to be small estates and a grant of probate or letters of administration are not necessary.

Some institutions, such as banks, building societies and insurance companies, state that they do not need a grant and that they can release the monies held once a release form has been drawn up. But be careful, for it is not as simple – or as cheap – as it first appears. First, there is a charge levied for this, usually a minimum of £30, and second, a fee per asset is charged for a release document.

On the other hand, to obtain a grant from the Probate Registry, from 26 April 1999, no fee is charged for estates under £5,000. While a release document is needed for each asset held by the various banks and insurance companies, only one grant of probate or letter of administration is needed and this document or official copies of it may be produced.

If, however, you do decide to use the service offered by these institutions you will have to make a declaration on the release form, usually before a solicitor or magistrate; this has to be done each time you complete one of the forms. Again, a charge is levied on each occasion. In addition, it is often necessary for all benefiting persons to sign the release document, whereas if done through the Probate Registry only one or possibly two persons need to be involved with the procedure.

'Excepted estates'

In its June 1991 press release the Inland Revenue stated that regulations in England and Wales 'have been laid to increase the limit for "excepted estates" to the limit of £125,000'. This has been increased from 5 April 1996 for deaths on or after 6 April 1996, to £180,000. This has been further increased to £200,000 for deaths after 5 April 1998. This means that executors or administrators of straightforward estates will not have to supply the estate's accounts provided that the following conditions have been met and the limit of the value of the total gross estate has not been exceeded. This limit applies to the aggregate gross value of the estate and of chargeable transfers of cash, quoted shares and securities within seven years *before* death. Excepted estates grant as mentioned here only refers to estates in England, Wales and Northern Ireland. The Inland Revenue claimed that this increase would simplify the administration of 7,500 small estates with regard to inheritance tax.

Estates qualify as 'excepted estates' only if all the following conditions are met:

1. The total value of the estate for tax purposes is not more than £200,000.
2. The estate comprises property that has passed under the deceased's will or intestacy or by nomination or by survivorship.[1]
3. Property outside the United Kingdom does not amount to more than £50,000 in value.
4. The deceased died domiciled in the United Kingdom and had not made lifetime gifts chargeable to either inheritance tax or capital transfer tax.
5. The total gross value of chargeable transfers of cash, quoted shares or securities within seven years *before* death has been introduced at a value of £75,000.

Estates do not qualify if the deceased had made a chargeable potentially exempt transfer or had made a gift with 'a reservation that subsists at the time of death or within seven years of the death'. Lastly, estates will not qualify if the deceased had an interest in settled property.

---

[1] If the value of an estate is attributable in part to property passes by survivorship in joint tenancy, then it is the value of the deceased's beneficial interest in that property that is taken into account for the purpose of valuation and the £200,000 limit.

These changes do not affect Scotland nor will the Lord Chancellor's Department in England and Wales be making changes to its Non-Contentious Probate Fees Order.

For readers wishing to know more about the changes of excepted estates, copies of the regulations are available from The Stationery Office by phoning the orderline number 0845 2341000.

What is a life interest?

Before making a will you would need to decide whether you will leave your house to your spouse in a life interest or whether you will leave it to him or her absolutely, in other words, without any conditions. If you decide on giving a life interest in the property, then your spouse would benefit from its use for the rest of his or her life, passing it on to other stated beneficiaries under the terms of your will upon death. Life interest in a property, for example, would mean that your spouse could live in or rent the property for the rest of his or her life but would not actually own it.

House repairs and maintenance would obviously need to be carried out at some time, so it would have to be decided by you whether the life interest beneficiary would pay for this or whether it would be paid for jointly by all the beneficiaries concerned. Rentals earned would go directly to the person who is benefiting from the life interest.

If the life interest involves money, your spouse would receive the interest that the capital sum earned but the capital would remain intact for the other beneficiaries upon his or her death. You would need to decide on the amount of acceptable interest, capital growth, or a mixture of both. Your decision would need to be included in your will. For stocks and shares, the life interest would entitle your spouse to the receipt of income (interest and dividends) but not the actual capital invested. Do specify the type of investment as otherwise it will be left to the discretion of the trustees.

The benefit of life interest is that your surviving spouse has the house and income for life and the children benefit thereafter. You direct who receives what. However, there is a minus side to it. First, your personal representative is not able to finalise the administration of the estate, and second, a life interest can be expensive to administer. Income tax forms, trust accounts and so on will have to be completed annually and perhaps a financial adviser brought in too. All these experts would charge fees for handling matters. The only other way would be to stipulate one type of investment to produce income, the other type to produce capital growth, and to ensure that your spouse receives all income. This would then go on his or her Tax Return and he or she would complete the Trust Tax Return also. So unless your estate is of sufficient size and value to warrant it, or you feel your children's rights should be safeguarded above everything in case your spouse remarries, a life interest should not be considered.

Absolute gift is simpler as it means leaving outright any possession you direct without stipulation to the named beneficiary. In fact this alternative is the more common, and cheaper, of the two.

4

What Can Affect Your Will?

There are three ways in which your will can be revoked or made inoperable. The first two are deliberate acts through choice. You can destroy your will or you can make a new will that includes a statement that you wish to revoke the earlier document. The third one applies in England and Wales: if you get married and do not specifically state in your will that after this event you wish your current will to remain in force, your marriage would invalidate the will.

Marriage

Let us take the unconscious act of invalidating a will, that is, through marriage. Scottish readers should see page 138 for the application of Scottish law. In England and Wales, to avoid invalidating your will by marriage, you can insert a statement to the effect that the will is to remain effective after your marriage to a specifically 'named' person. By doing this, the will is not revoked when you marry. So if you expect to marry a particular person at the time the will is made, then provided the following clause is inserted, any such will would still remain valid. But remember, you must name the person you intend to marry.

Example
'I [name] make this will in contemplation of my marriage to [name] and wish this will to remain in force after the said marriage.'

Divorce

If you divorce, under English law, then from the date of the decree absolute your former husband or wife will no longer benefit from your will and any gift made to him or her will lapse or be void. Unless you have made proper alternative provisions in your will to cover this eventuality the subject of the gift will be dealt with as if you had died intestate and may not pass in the manner that you would have wished. Moreover, it is possible that your ex-partner will administer the estate, in the role of guardian – on your children's behalf.

Your spouse is also entitled to half of any inheritance you may receive up until the date of your decree absolute. Thereafter, under English law, they are not entitled to receive a share unless specified in the will.

Revocation of a will

The making of a new will usually revokes a previous one provided a statement to this effect is placed in the will, namely 'I revoke all former wills and testamentary dispositions previously made by me.' Even if this statement is not included there will be an implied revocation of earlier wills if the later document clearly disposes of the whole estate.

Another instance where a will is naturally revoked is if it is deliberately destroyed by the person who has written it with the intention of revoking it. A will can also be destroyed by another person on the instructions of the testator but this must be done in his or her presence and under his or her direction, and the testator must intend that the will is to be revoked by such destruction. If this happens, the testator must categorically state to the third person present that it is his or her intention to destroy and revoke the will and then instruct that person to do so on his or her behalf.

Writing across the top of your will 'I revoke this will' does not mean that the will ceases to exist. You can, of course, accidentally destroy a will by destroying your own signature or that of your witnesses but unless the intention was there to revoke the will, legally it remains valid.

If a codicil accompanies a will and you later revoke that will by destruction, unless you also destroy the accompanying codicil it remains in force.

Legally, you cannot unintentionally destroy your will. If you lose it while moving house, the will is still considered to be legally in force and only by making out a new will revoking its predecessor will the old one be made void.

An example of assumed destruction of a will is if your executors cannot find it after your death although it is known that one had been made. If it was last known to have been in your possession, there is a legal presumption that it has been revoked by you. This presumption can be rebutted by evidence showing that there was definitely no intention to revoke the will.

A 'wish of intent'

To the best of human endeavours, the State intends that the persons named in your will should benefit from your property, according to the terms of your will. However, if the language of the will is ambiguous, then further investigation by the executor or, in some instances, the court may be called for. Evidence would have to be shown in order to try to interpret your wishes. This evidence can take the form of letters sent to your next of kin or conversations held with them when you expressed a 'wish of intent' or actions that indicate unchanged affection. They would have to swear that this was exactly what happened, however. Any falsification of evidence would be a serious matter indeed. This is why it is so important to express clearly what your intentions are.

Disputes and unknown factors

Suppose Great Uncle Harry dies without any issue, leaving you as his only descendant. If you had an argument and he decided not to leave you a legacy, under the Inheritance (Provision for Family and Dependants) Act 1975, you are able to apply to the court to be given part of Great Uncle Harry's estate. However, you would first have to establish that you were in some way a dependant of his. The court's powers are wide and in order to stand a chance of receiving any inheritance under the Act's provisions you would have to show that you were materially supported by him; for example, he let you live under his roof, gave you food and made sure that you were physically well cared for.

A further example of unknown factors overturning the wishes of a will is if you divorced and later married a divorcee who had a child. Then if you and your new wife in turn had a child and you forgot or intentionally failed to name either in your will, they would be able to put a claim in against your estate as they could be seen to be 'children of the family' and therefore dependants. Again, it is up to the discretion of the court to decide on the proportion of the estate, if any, to be paid out.

Another common wish inserted in wills that can cause disputes is one of continuous family inheritance. It has a moral implication rather than a legal one because of the Statute of Limitations, which means life plus 70 years. Also, you cannot dictate what another person does with his or her will. In cases such as this, you can make a gift of a life interest only to be passed back to the estate upon death and then on to the next stated beneficiary.

Although it would not make your will invalid if you state in it that you wish your eldest child to have a certain item and in turn he or she is instructed to pass this item on to his or her eldest child, it might not occur. So despite the fact that they are under a moral duty to do this, there is no legal obligation.

You cannot stipulate in your will that your house must be lived in by your son if it inflicts separation between parent and child or instigates the intention of breaking up a marriage. Such clauses are deemed to be 'contrary to public policy' and the law ensures that such stipulations do not stand. The same applies to religion. You cannot stipulate in your will that your grandchildren (or any other person) be brought up in a particular religious faith in order to inherit from your estate. To insert a clause stating that a child will be excluded from a legacy if he is brought up in a religion other than his own would be to invalidate that section of your will. Again, it is seen as contrary to public policy. The definition of a specific religion is also seen as too vague and extensive clarification would be needed.

The term 'contrary to public policy' can be seen in many different ways and nowadays will often be discarded because the phrase itself is too vague. It is supposed to reflect what is believed to be public policy at the present time.

Courts can, once petitioned, examine the disposition of gifts within the will if those gifts are regarded as 'contrary to public policy'. However, in such instances it is up to the court on the day to decide on the individual merit of each case. Therefore, it is not possible to expand further within the terms of this book. A solicitor should be consulted where such a situation arises.

Making a gift void

Wills may be declared invalid if it is proved that they were made as a result of excessive pestering, in other words if someone tried to persuade you to leave everything you own (or even a specific gift) to them. So, if a person has imposed undue influence on you, and this can be proved, the will can be seen as invalid.

If a murder was committed by a beneficiary of a will (or indeed the beneficiary aided and abetted somebody in causing the death of the testator), regardless of the benefits noted in the will the murderer or accomplice would receive no inheritance. In committing the crime he or she automatically forfeits his or her right to inherit. Incidentally, it is also possible that a person found guilty of manslaughter in a motor accident which caused the death of the testator, who under the terms of the deceased's will was left an inheritance, could forfeit his or her legacy.

A condition attached to a gift in the will that requires the beneficiary to commit an unlawful act of whatever nature is not recognised and the gift will usually be paid without regard to the condition. Of course, whether this is a statement in a will or not, the request is illegal.

You should not ask a beneficiary or the spouse of a beneficiary to witness your will because in so doing you are making the gift void.

Overall, it should be remembered that generally, unless a person has a valid claim, the courts do not as a rule turn aside the testator's wishes. The invalidation of your will, therefore, is not a matter that should worry you unduly.

Rules to follow

To ensure that you make a valid will there are a few rules to follow. First, you must be over 18 years of age, and second, you must sign the will in the presence of two witnesses both of whom must be present at the same time. Those witnesses must then, before leaving your presence, sign their names at the bottom of the document. There is another requirement. You must also be mentally capable of understanding your actions and know what you are doing, and intending to do, when signing your will.

There is an exception to the age requirement noted above. A person over 14 but under 18 can make a will, provided that the person is on active military service in times of war. Similarly, seamen at sea in peacetime may also exercise this privilege.

It cannot be stressed too often that a will must clearly state your intentions, in other words exactly who is to receive precisely what. Many a confusion occurs and many a will is made invalid because the instructions are not clear.

'All my property' means just that – absolutely everything you own. You might have wanted the house to go to your spouse and perhaps some of your personal effects; also, you may have wanted a few mementoes to go to your son, mother or friend. With the use of the above phrase, they would receive nothing.

Another stumbling block when a will is being written by a layperson is the over-indulgent use of what are considered to be legal phrases. Again, you may think you meant one thing but, in fact, it would be judged as something entirely different. For example, 'I leave all my money' means, 'I leave you all my cash', nothing else, just cash in its physical form and in bank and building society accounts. It does not include the value of the house, furnishings or any other valuable you own or, indeed, even the value that any such items could realise. Keep the phrases simple and specific, and select your words carefully.

The main tasks of the Probate Registry are to decide on the validity of a will and to interpret it for the purpose of deciding who to appoint as personal representatives. Unclear statements can cause problems when it comes to making this interpretation. In 1988 new Non-Contentious Probate Rules were introduced giving the Registrar some discretion as to enquiries that could be made with regard to establishing the validity of a will. This book cannot possibly cover all these considerations; whether or not you have written the will yourself, you should check to make sure that your will has been prepared correctly.

Basically, the Registrar cannot alter the distribution arrangements as laid out in the will, although if it becomes clear that there has been some mistake in the wording because of a misunderstanding he or she may, on behalf of the testator, put the mistake right provided all persons affected by this action agree to it. However, the will's intentions cannot be altered: so if monies are given, then all cash is inherited; if a house is given, then the property is passed on; and if 'all that I own' is given, then everything the deceased owned must be passed on. Of course, if a spouse, son or daughter or, indeed, any person who claims to be a dependant, is excluded, they can apply to the court and ask to be awarded part of the estate.

A will is accepted as valid in England and Wales without query if it appears to be signed properly and has a clause called an *attestation clause* inserted in it. (Printed wills obtained from stationers have this clause.) This clause confirms that the necessary rules have been followed when a person signs the will. If it has not been inserted, enquiries will usually have to be made to confirm that the will was properly signed.

In England and Wales an unsigned will is invalid but in Scotland (see Chapter 11) a *holograph* (written in the person's own hand) will is not necessarily invalid because it is not signed. Alteration made to a will after it has been properly signed may also invalidate it, and such amendments will not take effect unless the will is signed and witnessed again. Sometimes minor alterations do occur and provided that this happens before the will is signed, the incorrect word or line should be crossed out and the substitute one written above it. At the time the will is signed and witnessed you should place your initials alongside the altered text. The witnesses must also place their initials alongside the alterations.

The best rule to follow, however, should be that if alterations are necessary, then make out a new will. Only minor alterations should be inserted in the form of a codicil. A codicil acts as an insertion in your will; for example, the amended distribution of a particular item.

It does not matter what your will has been written on provided that the Registrar sees that it is a fair copy. Registrars are used to receiving all manner of wills, from those written on brown paper to, on occasions, those written on tracing paper – although such a presentation is not recommended.

5

How To Write a Will

One of the greatest problems facing the Probate Registry is unclear meaning in the wording in many 'home-made' wills. While there is sufficient leeway for the Registrar to make an interpretation, in some cases this is not possible and the will then has to have its meaning defined in accordance with the rules, possibly in a higher court, namely the Chancery Court. The courts try to decipher what the deceased may have wanted to say, but a precise interpretation may not be possible because of the unclear wording. Any ambiguity, whether in the usage of a word or phrase, must be avoided. This rule applies even if a solicitor is drawing up your will as it has been known for them to make mistakes too. For example, a gift of your possessions held 'in' your property means held in your abode, while held 'in and on' means both in the house and on the property's plot. If prepared for you, then read your will to ensure it says what you mean to happen.

When writing your will you must state clearly, using full names, who is to receive the gift as well as giving a full description of the item or items named. For example, if you have two antique button-back chairs and you want your favourite niece to receive one, then describe the chair precisely. Give the colour of the upholstery, trim and any small detail that can help in identifying the chair, and your niece's full name and current or last known address.

Checklist for your will

On a separate sheet of paper you should note what assets you have and whom you wish to benefit. When looking at the valuation of your estate (see the checklist example on this page), make sure that it is not going to attract more inheritance tax than at first anticipated. If it is, you should take steps to examine how this liability can be lessened (see Chapters 6 and 7).

You will need to state in your will whether your individual beneficiaries have to pay inheritance tax from their legacy or whether you wish all legacies to be paid in full and any tax due to be taken out of the balance of the residue of the estate. If you have any outstanding debts, perhaps a loan from the bank or a mortgage, this should also be noted in your lists so that your calculations of these debts can be deducted from its total. Remember, whatever route you decide to take, tax usually has to be paid before probate is granted. A loan can be obtained from a bank to raise the tax money and the interest from the loan can be deducted from the estate's value when calculating the total inheritance tax liability. However, although this route speeds up the process in that the grant may be obtained quickly, it is not the best route to take as the interest still has to be paid and, although deducted from tax due, it is not 100 per cent relievable, ie you still pay 60 per cent in the pound. Another route for payment of tax is if the estate holds any National Savings monies or premium bonds; then your solicitor or, if you are making a personal application, the Probate Registry, can organise with these authorities for the taxable amount to be deducted from such holdings.

A checklist of assets should now be drafted. For a more comprehensive list of items for inclusion see the Estate Checklist in Chapter 11, pages 133–34.

Example 1. Checklist of assets of A. N. Other

Item			Amount
			£
House	value	£100,000	
	less mortgage	£40,000	60,000
Life insurance with [name] Co Ltd			
	on death worth		60,000
Pension with [name] Co Ltd			
	on death worth		40,000

Current value of shares and unit trusts held	5,000
Building society accounts	
[name] Building Society (1)	1,500
[name] Building Society (2)	1,900
Bank accounts with [name]	
current	750
deposit	5,000
Second-hand value of car	2,500
Half of furnishings and personal effects	5,000
Approximate total	£181,650

Example 2. Notes for legacy in, [name], will

1. My wife, [name], is to have the house, car, money in the building society and bank accounts [names and account numbers], furnishings except for those listed below, half the proceeds of my life insurance policy with [insurance company's name] and the residue of my estate.
2. My children, [name] and [name], to receive half of the proceeds from my pensions policy with [insurance company's name], half the proceeds of my life insurance with [insurance company's name] to be held in trust with my wife as trustee.
3. To my brother, [name], half of the value of my shares and unit trusts and my Hornby train set.
4. To my mother, [name], half of the value of my shares and unit trusts and my gold fob watch with chain.
5. To my friends, [name] and [name], the gate-legged oak table with inlaid top.
6. If my wife dies before me, ask my brother, [name], to set up a trust and act on the children's behalf until they reach the age of 21.

In this example, the estate is valued at over £181,650, so estate planning would not be needed if you died after 6 April 2000.

Before moving on to the writing of a will and different examples of clauses that can be inserted, it is worth noting that you are able to purchase a printed will form from any of the large high street stationers. However, there is not a great deal of space allowed for the provision of various legacies and additional sheets would have to be inserted.

When writing your own will there is one clause that must always be included. Many a new will is written and the old one is forgotten or ignored. The phrase which should be inserted in every new will is, 'I revoke all former wills and codicils and testamentary provisions.' If you make a new will forgetting to destroy the earlier one, and if this *revocation clause* is not included, the latter will may not prevail in its entirety. On occasions when this happens both documents have to be proved and the combined provisions, provided they are not inconsistent with each other, are applied.

Always keep a carbon copy or a photocopy of your will whether it is handwritten or typed. Do ensure that your executor(s) know its location.

The following checklist of sentences appear in sequence in any will. The letters at the start of each sentence refer to the example of a will to be found on pages 61–63 and to further inclusions which are found on pages 63–66.

(A) A will should always start with the sentence 'This is the last will and testament of [name]'.

(B) This statement is followed by your full name, your full current address and the date that the will is being made.

(C) A statement revoking all previous wills and codicils and testamentary provisions is inserted next.

(D) A statement appointing your executors and noting whether any payment is to be made to them.

(E) If you have any particular wishes, such as funeral arrangements, these wishes should be inserted next.

(F) A statement needs to be included to the effect that all estate expenses incurred (known as *testamentary expenses*) should be paid by the estate. Also this section should state whether the gifts made in the will are to be free of inheritance tax liability. If this is the case, you will have to allow for the correct amount when first preparing your estate valuation.

(G) Now you list any specific gifts of money (known as *pecu-niary legacies*) in detail, stating who is to receive what amount. The following statement should be made for each gift. 'I give and bequeath the following legacy to [name] of [address]'. If you wish these legacies to be paid from a particular fund you should state this by inserting 'payable from my deposit account in [name] Bank plc'.

(H) After (G), the following statement listing other legacies is inserted for each gift. 'I give and bequeath the following to [name] of [address]'. Note carefully what gift is to be received and if it is, say, a house or a piece of land, then note the exact location.

(I)   You should end your will with a clause disposing of those assets that you have not as yet given to anyone. The *residue* or remainder of the estate would go to this person once all debts (inheritance tax, funeral expenses and so on) have been paid. A suitable clause would be: 'I [name] of [address] devise and bequeath the residue of my real and personal estate'.

In addition, a *survivorship clause* should be inserted stating that should this main beneficiary not survive you by 30 days the residue of the estate should go to another named person. This is done to clarify any possible claim by beneficiaries from either side should, for example, both husband and wife die in the same accident where the precise time of death could not be established. If the husband died in an accident and 10 days later his main beneficiary, ie his wife, also died, the residue of his estate which was being left to her would go to his other substituted chief beneficiary. Without this clause the husband's estate would have been given across to his wife's estate for distribution according to the bequests of her will or the rules of intestacy governing her estate.

(J)   This statement is followed by what is known as the *attestation clause*. 'Signed by the said testator in the presence of us, present at the same time and by us in his presence.' Here you may sign either beside the clause or below it and the signatures of your two witnesses also appear here, below your signature. Each witness should also write his or her full current address. (Remember, neither a beneficiary of the will nor the spouse of a beneficiary may witness the will. In such an event, the gift is forfeit.)

As individual needs and circumstances differ, so each will and its content will reflect these differences. A married man with a wife and child will want to ensure that they are well provided for. An elderly person who has no close relatives would perhaps want to leave his or her estate not only to relatives but to charity or friends. A single person, with perhaps a brother or sister, will have different priorities and the same would apply to a widow or widower. The sample will that follows allows for the adoption of different clauses which different people may want to include. The letters in brackets relate to the previous list of statements that should appear in a will.

Example of a will

(A) THIS IS THE LAST WILL AND TESTAMENT OF (B) Edith Mary Baker of Somerset Farm, Non-Such Lane, Burton, Warwickshire made this fifth day of October one thousand nine hundred and ninety-seven.

(C) I hereby revoke all former wills, codicils or other testamentary provisions at any time made by me and declare this to be my last will.

(D) I appoint my husband, James Arthur Baker of Somerset Farm, Non-Such Lane, Burton, Warwickshire and my son Richard John Baker of Rose Cottage, Hill Street, Minford, Warwickshire and Mr J Blogham of J Blogham and Sons, High Street, Minford, Warwickshire to be the executors of my will and Mr J Blogham shall be entitled to charge and to be paid for all professional or any other charges for any business or acts done by him in connection with this will.

(E) I express the wish that my body be buried in the graveyard at Burton Church and devise and bequeath the sum of £500 to the said church.

(F) All gifts are subject to the payment of my just debts, funeral and testamentary expenses and all taxes and duties payable.

(G) I devise and bequeath to each of my grandchildren Robert Matthew Baker and Amanda Mary Baker of Rose Cottage, Hill Street, Minford, Warwickshire who shall be living at the time of my death the sum of £2,000.

I give and bequeath the sum of £1,500 to the Burton Dogs Home, Mile End Lane, Burton, Warwickshire.

(H) I give and bequeath my half share of the freehold land and property of Somerset Farm, Non-Such Lane, Burton, Warwickshire to my son Richard John Baker of Rose Cottage, Hill Street, Minford, Warwickshire or if this should be sold or otherwise disposed of during my lifetime any other land or property owned by me at the date of my death free and discharged from all sums secured thereon by way of mortgage or otherwise absolutely.

I devise and bequeath to my daughter-in-law Mary Anne Baker of Rose Cottage, Hill Street, Minford, Warwickshire my emerald and diamond engagement ring, the oak grandmother clock with brass fixtures standing in the hall of my home, the brooch shaped as an apple with five diamonds, and the sum of £5,000.

I devise and bequeath to my grandson Robert Matthew Baker of Rose Cottage, Hill Street, Minford, Warwickshire my stamp collection absolutely.

I devise and bequeath to my granddaughter Amanda Mary Baker of Rose Cottage, Hill Street, Minford, Warwickshire, the remainder of my jewellery not previously disposed of.

I devise and bequeath to my sister Mrs Emily Mary Lewis of 22 Mill Lane, Burton, Warwickshire the sum of £5,000, and the picture entitled 'Roses in Bloom' painted by William Lewis and currently hanging in the hall of my house.

(I) I devise and bequeath the residue and remainder of my estate both real and personal to my husband James Arthur Baker of Somerset Farm, Non-Such Lane, Burton, Warwickshire absolutely if he shall survive me by thirty days. If he shall not survive me by thirty days then I devise and bequeath all the residue and remainder of my real and personal estate whatsoever and wheresoever to be divided equally among those of my grandchildren whosoever shall be living at the date of my death.

(J) In witness hereof I have set my hand this day and year first written.

Edith Mary Baker [signature]

Signed by the said testator in the presence of us present at the same time and by us in her presence

Catherine Mary Brown [signature]
High Street,
Burton,
Warwickshire
(Solicitor)

John Henry Willis [signature]
High Street,
Burton,
Warwickshire
(Solicitor)

Notes

1. If you were going to appoint only, say, a firm of solicitors as executors, the first paragraph would have to read:

'I appoint the partners at the date of my death in the firm of Messrs Blogham and Sons of High Street, Minford, Warwickshire (hereinafter called my trustees) to be executors of this my will. The executors and trustees shall be entitled to charge [insert charge if necessary] and be paid out of the residue of my estate all professional and other charges for all business or acts done by them in connection with this my will.'

Do, however, ask any professionals what charges they are likely to make against a current will, as an exact figure for some time in the future could not possibly be given. If it is to be a percentage of the value of the estate, you can insert this figure in the appropriate space as noted above.

2. If your children were to be the sole beneficiaries of your estate, you would need to insert the following clause immediately after the executor's clause (D).

'I devise and bequeath all my real and personal estate whatsoever and wheresoever to my children [name] of [address] and [name] of [address] absolutely if they shall survive me by thirty days.'

You would also need to insert the provision that should your main and sole beneficiaries not survive you by 30 days you would leave your estate to someone else. An example of this would be:

'If they shall not survive me by thirty days I devise and bequeath all my said estate whatsoever and wheresoever to [name] of [address] absolutely or in the event of him [or her] not surviving me for the aforesaid period I direct that my said estate is [insert here what you wish to do with your estate in these circumstances].'

3. In the event that you wish to leave a life interest to your husband, for example, then the following paragraph should be inserted in the will in place of the paragraph after the executor's clause (D). As life interest clauses can cause disharmony because they are restrictive, careful consideration needs to be given before inserting one.

'I devise and bequeath all my real and personal estate whatsoever and wheresoever to my trustees upon trust to sell (to postpone sale) and to invest the proceeds thereof and apply the income for the benefit of my husband [name] of [address] until he dies or remarries whichever is the sooner. Thereafter in the event of his death or remarriage the proceeds are to be divided among such of my children [names] of [addresses] as shall be living at the date of my husband's death or remarriage absolutely.'

As you can see from the sample will, you can make as many and as varied 'dispositions' as you wish, provided that you clearly state that you 'give and bequeath' or 'devise and bequeath' whatever legacy you wish to give and to whom.

Presuming that you wish to make various gifts but that the remainder of your estate is to be divided between your husband and son, in other words neatly cutting the residue of your estate in half, the following clause would need to be inserted at (I).

'I devise and bequeath half of my real and personal estate whatsoever and wheresoever to my husband [name] of [address] absolutely if he shall survive me by thirty days and the other half of my real and personal estate whatsoever and wheresoever to my son [name] of [address] in equal shares absolutely. If either one shall not survive me by thirty days then his share shall accrue to my estate and be given absolutely to the survivor.'

If you are a widow or widower with a child under the age of eighteen, you may wish to take this age factor into account and insert the following clause (instead of (F)).

'I devise and bequeath all my real and personal estate whatsoever and wheresoever to my trustees [names and addresses] upon trust to pay my funeral and testamentary expenses and to stand in possession of the residue of my estate and apply the income therefrom for the benefit of my son [name] of [address] until he reaches the age of twenty-one and thereafter to him absolutely.'

It would be prudent, in case of a tragedy, to insert the following statement underneath the one noted above in case the minor should also not survive but leave children.

'I devise and bequeath all my real and personal estate whatsoever and wheresoever to my son [name] of [address] and in the event of his death before me for his share to pass to such of his children who shall be living at the time of my death.'

As you can see in the main will, when leaving a legacy to a relative, it is best that you specify what that relationship is. So, for example, if the person is a half sister, the will should specify this relationship, ie 'to my sister of the half blood'. Always try to give the full and correct names of beneficiaries rather than 'pet' names and always give the last known (or current) address.

When leaving money to charities, note clearly the full name and correct address of that charity along with the bequests that you desire to make. Often charities, knowing that you wish to contribute, will supply you with a separate legacy form. It is not, however, advisable to use this unless it is your intention that the charity should benefit absolutely. Instead, include the legacy with the others in your will.

If you are a partner in a business, this fact should be noted in the will and reference made to a partnership agreement, which should have been drawn up on the commencement of that business. This agreement should stipulate the precise division of the firm's shares or your interest. In a two-man partnership, if one partner dies leaving the other half of the business (noted as his property) to his wife, the surviving partner has two options. First, he can agree to buy out the deceased partner's share, or second, he can take his partner's spouse in as a new partner. If the latter instance occurs, a new partnership document must be drawn up. In the case of the former, the surviving partner would have to have sufficient funds available to buy out the wife's share. Of course, the partnership agreement can include contingency plans to ensure that the surviving partner keeps the business afloat.

Lastly, if you wish to leave your body or parts of your body for medical research or for transplant surgery, in addition to carrying a donor card, you can insert the following clause, at (E). Of course, do notify your next of kin of this wish.

'I desire and authorise after my death the use of part [state which] (or parts) of my body for medical research.'

What is a codicil?

When making a simple alteration to your will or when revoking any provision made in it, a codicil can be used. If you wish to change executors or to name a person not previously included as a beneficiary in your will, again a codicil can be used.

By adding this supplement to your will you can include new instructions and delete old ones without having to go through the task of rewriting the whole of the will.

You can make as many codicils as you wish. However, too many might make your affairs complicated and it might be easier and simpler to rewrite your will. As a rule, if any matter is not straightforward, a new will should be written rather than relying on a codicil.

To be valid a codicil has to be signed by yourself and witnessed (not necessarily by the original witnesses of your will) in exactly the same way as your will. Again, as with your will, these witnesses must not be beneficiaries of your will nor must their spouses be named.

A codicil takes the following form:

I [name] of [address] declare this to be a first [or second or third, etc] codicil to my will dated that fifth day of October one thousand nine hundred and ninety-seven.

I revoke the previous bequest to my neighbour Mrs Sally Seward of 22 Highcliffe Road, Weston on Sea of £500 and I in turn give £500 to Mrs Lucy May Smith of 13 Sellwright Road, Weston on Sea.

In all other respects I confirm my will.

This codicil is dated the twenty-second day of January one thousand nine hundred and ninety-eight.
Signed by [testator's signature]

Signed by the said testator in our presence and then by us in his presence

(Here the witnesses sign their names giving their full addresses and occupations.)

David Smith, High Street, Weston on Sea (Shopkeeper)

Phillip Lewis, Seacliffe, Burton on Sea (Retired Naval Officer)

If you do make a codicil, ensure that you refer to your will, stating the correct date of that will.

6

A Question of Tax

In his 1986 Budget the Chancellor officially changed the name of capital transfer tax to that of inheritance tax. A further but more fundamental change took place in his 1988 Budget with regard to capital taxes in the United Kingdom. From 15 March 1988 whoever lived in the United Kingdom would have their estate – upon death – taxed once assets exceeded £110,000 (current rate for 2000–01 is £234,000). Any monies over that amount would be applicable to a single band of inheritance tax at the rate of 40 per cent.

This change drastically reduced the potential liability that existed before that date on the larger estates. Therefore this has to be a prime motivator in replanning your estate to take full advantage of the current state of tax planning. For example, before the 1988 Budget a widow with assets of £700,000 would have paid £326,000 in inheritance tax on her death. The example below assumes that she had made no gifts over the past seven years.

	£
House	250,000
Stocks and shares	300,000
Personal effects	100,000
Building society deposits	50,000
Total value of estate	700,000

In tax terminology, gifts are meant as a sum of money or a portion of her estate given to anyone before her death.

Provided that seven years had elapsed from the time of making a gift until her death, then no tax would be payable on the value of that gift. If death occurred during that period, then a portion of tax would be payable on the value of the gift (see Table 6.3).

Table 6.1 – Prior to 15 March 1988

Cumulative chargeable transfer	Rate of tax	Tax on band	Cumulative tax
0–£90,000	nil	nil	nil
£90,001–£140,000	30%	£15,000	£15,000
£140,001–£200,000	40%	£24,000	£39,000
£200,001–£330,000	50%	£65,000	£104,000
£330,001–£700,000	60%	£222,000	£326,000

Effective rate of tax £326,000/£700,000 × 100 = 46.57 per cent.

Since 15 March 1988, inheritance tax has gradually been reduced so that now for deaths after 6 April 1999, it means a reduction of 19 per cent. This would be calculated as follows:

Table 6.2 – After 15 March 1988 at current 2000/01 rates

Cumulative chargeable transfer	Rate of tax	Tax on band	Cumulative tax
0–£234,000	nil	nil	nil
£234,001–£700,000	40%	£186,399	£186,399

Effective rate of tax £186,399/£700,000 × 100 = 26.63 per cent.

Currently any personal gifts made during a person's lifetime in excess of the annual or other specific exemptions, such as gifts on marriage, are known as potentially exempt transfers or PETS for short. These transfers are subject to inheritance tax only if the person who makes the gift dies within a seven-year period from the time of making the gift. Tax is reduced on a sliding scale depending on how many years have elapsed before the donor's death. The following table shows you what that timescale is:

Table 6.3

Years before death	Percentage of death rate (%)
0–3	100
3–4	80
4–5	60
5–6	40
6–7	20

It cannot be stressed too often that sensible tax planning is urged for those individuals with estates still within reach of the Inland Revenue. For the sake of a few hundred pounds spent now, it could save your estate thousands later. Planning now reduces adverse effects later, whether or not these changes are governmental or from a premature death.

Equalisation of estates

The first basic step for the planning of an estate, assuming you are married, is equalisation of the estate between husband and wife. Each spouse should leave at least the amount of the nil rate band (currently £234,000) directly to their children, close relatives (other than husband or wife) or indeed to a close friend, assuming, of course, that the estate's value is greater than the threshold. There is a proviso and that is: should this gift be made, would the surviving spouse have sufficient monies with which to live financially? So what must be upmost in your mind is for both spouses to use the amount allowed for in the nil rate band.

Take the following example. A couple have a combined estate of £320,000. Should the husband die first and leave all his money to his wife who, sadly, dies six months later, on the value of the estate, tax of £34,400 would have to be paid. No tax would be payable on the first death as transfers between husband and wife are exempt. However, on her death the following calculation applies:

Table 6.4

Estate	£320,000			
Tax	£34,400			
Transfer	Slice	Rate	Tax on slice	Total tax
0–£234,000	£234,000	0%	nil	nil
£234,001–£320,000	£85,999	40%	£34,399	£34,399

Effective rate £34,400/£320,000 × 100 = 10.75 per cent.

Because of this charge you might be tempted to say 'there is now no need to plan for inheritance tax'. But if you are in the fortunate position as shown in Table 6.2 of having that amount of assets, effectively you will be writing your will as 'to my friends and relatives I leave £513,601 and to the government I leave £186,399'. You may, of course, feel generously inclined to the tax authorities, but 40 per cent still bites deep into anyone's estate!

On the other hand, in Table 6.4, had the husband and wife planned their estate and the husband had left £234,000 to his son with the balance of £86,000 to his wife, no tax would be paid on his death and no tax would be payable on the death of his wife six months later.

Equalisation of assets between spouses not only saves on inheritance tax but, if a future government were ever to introduce an annual wealth tax or decrease the threshold and/or the percentage level at which the difference is paid on, equalisation would minimise the effect of this tax as well.

No matter what you decide on, eventually the government will change and the question of capital taxes – limits and/or methods of calculation – will probably be cause for thought once more. The need therefore exists to plan your estate effectively if you think that it will exceed the current tax band. Remember, of course, that this band depends on the Chancellor's discretion and the amount will no doubt be adjusted in subsequent Budgets.

'But my estate isn't going to exceed £234,000.' When was the last time you valued all your possessions? What is the current value of your house? Have you recently taken out an addition to your life insurance policy? Have you increased your pension contributions? Has an endowment policy recently been paid? What savings and investments do you now hold? Have you received any windfall shares? Leaving aside the possibility of you being a beneficiary of someone else's estate, does your revised calculation now show your estate to be worth over £234,000? Many people revising the value of their assets are pleasantly surprised. 'It won't be any problem, I won't have to pay the tax.' But your estate will and, after all, the estate is yours.

Settlements

Instead of using outright gifts to reduce the value of your estate you may instead prefer to use *settlements*. It was the 1986 Finance Act that introduced inheritance tax, which replaced the old capital transfer tax. Under this new Act, gifts made into *accumulation and maintenance settlements* or gifts into *interest in possession trusts* are, as with outright gifts, seen as 'potentially exempt transfers' or PETS, which means there is no inheritance tax liability, provided the person making a gift survives a period of seven years after making the settlement.

If you have children, or indeed if you have grandchildren, accumulation and maintenance settlements are especially suitable. Under this type of settlement the beneficiary will receive income from the trust as a right and by the age of 25 receives the entire holding. There are certain rules to follow when considering making this settlement and these are:

1. The beneficiary is entitled to the property of the trust or to an interest in possession on attaining a specified age, which must not exceed 25;
2. The income from the trust must either be accumulated within the fund or applied for the benefit of the beneficiary; and
3. Either:
    (a) not more than 25 years have elapsed since the settlement was first made, or
    (b) all the beneficiaries are grandchildren of a common grandparent.

Provided that these conditions can be satisfied, all gifts made into the trust are seen as 'potentially exempt transfers' and escape the periodic charge applicable to large *discretionary trusts*. An additional benefit is that there is no inheritance tax charge when the beneficiaries finally inherit all the assets. Of course, once you have made the gift, you cannot benefit or have the gift back or use that gift – unless in the case of a house, you pay a market rent.

There is, as with most things, a minus side. This downside is that if any of the beneficiaries are your own children under the age of 18 and receive income from the settlement in excess of £100 per annum, this income is added to your own and you in turn are liable to tax, potentially at the top rate of 40 per cent.

The use of *small discretionary settlements* can be most beneficial. These settlements provide a greater degree of flexibility on the distribution of income and capital, provided that the initial amount settled into them is less than the nil inheritance tax rate band. There is no inheritance tax to pay upon setting up the trust. A *discretionary trust* is one of the few areas of tax planning that does give rise to a lifetime charge[2] if the amount settled exceeds a person's chargeable nil rate band, but the tax payable is at half the death rate, in other words 20 per cent.

Of all the taxes applied throughout the United Kingdom, inheritance tax is the one which, provided careful planning has been done early enough, can be legally avoided.

Each year everyone is allowed an annual tax exemption of £3,000 per person against capital gifts. If you do not take advantage of this annual exemption, it remains available to be carried forward, but only for a further 12 months. It is therefore important to use this annual exemption each year. Other tax exemptions are noted on the following pages.

Transfers between husband and wife

The transfer of assets upon death between husband and wife, provided that the recipient is domiciled in the United Kingdom, is exempt from inheritance tax. If a person is not domiciled here, then only £55,000 is exempt.

[2] A lifetime charge – as opposed to a death charge – is one that is raised for payment during your lifetime.

Domicile

The understanding of the tax definition of the word 'domicile' is important, although it is a concept of general law and not tax law.

Your domicile is the place which you regard as your permanent home and which you consider to be the country with which you are most clearly connected and, if abroad, can be the place you intend to return to. You can only be domiciled in one place at a time and must positively establish your domicility by setting foot in the country concerned. To make matters more complicated there are three different domiciles: domicile of origin, domicile of choice and domicile of dependency.

Domicile of origin usually follows that of your father at the time of your birth, unless your father had died. If this had happened, then you would take on the domicile of your mother. Illegitimate children usually take the domicile of their mother.

Domicile of choice is the choosing of a new country to live in and to make your new life in – having permanently and *absolutely* abandoned the old country – and having no intention of returning to your old home.

You can have numerous domiciles of choice throughout your life provided that in each case you abandon the old place of domicile with the intention of permanently making your home in the new country of domicile and actually going to live there.

Domicile of dependency means that if you have a child under the age of 16 (or a mentally handicapped child), that child takes on the domicile of the person on whom he or she is dependent. You are deemed domiciled if you have lived in the United Kingdom after 9 December 1974; for taxation purposes you retain domicile status in the United Kingdom for three years after establishing domicile elsewhere. The tax authorities also deem you 'domiciled' if you have lived in the United Kingdom for most of the past 20 years of tax assessments.

Gifts

Small gifts
The outright gift to any one person of up to the value of £250 is exempt from tax.

Expenditure out of income

This can sometimes be difficult to establish as not only does the transfer have to come out of your normal expenditure but there must also be an element of regularity. In other words, if ever you give it bi-monthly, then this procedure must be kept up. The premiums for a life policy that have been written under trust, for example, will be treated as a gift for the purpose of inheritance tax, unless it can be shown that it falls within the normal expenditure rules as a gift out of income. To qualify under this exemption it has to come out of your 'after tax' income and still leave you with enough money to maintain yourself in your usual mode of living.

Gifts in consideration of marriage

This is limited to £5,000 if the donor is a parent of one of the marriage partners. It reduces to £2,500 if the donor is a grand-parent of either of the marriage partners and again reduces to £1,000 if the gift is from anyone else. These gifts must be made *before* the wedding ceremony.

Gifts to charities

There is no limit to the amount of money that can be donated to a registered charity free of tax.

Gifts to political parties

Again, there is no limit to the amount that can be donated to a political party provided that the party has at least two current sitting Members of Parliament or has polled not less than 150,000 votes for its candidates at the last general election.

Gifts for the public's benefit or for national purposes

There is no limit to the amount of money that can be donated, tax free, for these purposes.

By taking advantage of these exemptions, even if there were to be a change in government, gifts that were made at the time of exemptions should prove to be safe from any later changes that might be legislated.

When is inheritance tax applied?

Inheritance tax, if you are domiciled in the United Kingdom, or deemed to be domiciled, applies at death to all your property wherever it is situated globally once your assets exceed £234,000, current level. If you are not domiciled here, then inheritance tax will only apply to your assets which are situated in the United Kingdom. Assets mean property as well as personal effects with a quantifiable value.

Domicile

It is important to know whether you are deemed to be domiciled in the United Kingdom for inheritance tax purposes. The taxation officials have certain rules which apply to the definition of the term domicile. They are:

1. You are domiciled here on or after 10 December 1974 and within three years preceding death.
2. You are resident here on or before 10 December 1974 and in not less than 17 years of the previous 20 years.

The Isle of Man and the Channel Islands, for the purpose of inheritance tax, are not part of the United Kingdom, but all other parts, Scotland, Northern Ireland, Wales and England are taxed under the same rules.

Domicile – future changes

A new domicile bill had been expected which would have altered the domicile rules, making it easier for a person to change his domicile of origin. Unfortunately, in May 1993 the government said it had no immediate plans to change the law. It is reasonable to expect changes in the future.

To change one's domicile is not an easy matter as you are actually born with a domicility and, as previously stated, normally that is considered to be the same domicile as your father. In order to change your domicile to one of *domicile of choice* you have to have resided in your new chosen country for a considerable period of time, having proved an intent to live there by purchasing a new home. It also helps to marry a native of that country and to develop business interests there. Arrangements should be made so that your body is buried in that country and indeed that all connections with your former country of domicile be severed, even down to club membership.

Funeral expenses and any debts owed by you at the time of your death are deducted from the value of your estate before calculating the amount of tax payable. Tax must be paid before probate is granted.

Double taxation relief is available if some of the deceased's estate included some foreign property and a foreign tax, similar to inheritance tax, has been paid. Relief can be deducted up to the maximum amount of United Kingdom inheritance tax payable on the same assets. To calculate the amount of relief, you will need to find out the exact equivalent in pounds sterling of the foreign tax paid.

What can be achieved if no prior planning has been done?

Deed of variation

If someone has died within a two-year period, then their will can effectively be rewritten to take advantage of the £234,000 nil rate inheritance tax band. This is done by means of a document called 'a deed of family arrangement'. This document is a very valuable tool in inheritance tax planning, but it has to be remembered that:

(a) it can only be made within two years of a person's death;
(b) the Inland Revenue must be notified within six months from the date of variation;
(c) the deed of variation cannot be made if any of the legacies under the terms of the will have actually been disposed of; and
(d) all beneficiaries must agree to this being done.

Indeed, the prime reason for using a deed of variation or deed of family arrangement is because the estate in its present form is not tax efficient and a deed is made to make it more tax efficient.

Before having a deed of variation drawn up all the beneficiaries under the will must get together for common purpose and agree to the terms of the will. For example, suppose you die leaving the bulk of your estate to your wife but with the stipulation that upon her death a small portion is to go to one of her cousins. Because she is the sole beneficiary of your will your wife can amend it. You will certainly need the services of a solicitor in drawing up a deed.

The deed of variation takes its name because you are varying the terms of the will. Once a deed of variation has been accepted it is, in effect, taken as the ultimate varied will for tax purposes and treated as if it were the original one.

The Inland Revenue has four rules that must be observed before a deed of variation is accepted.

1. A notice in writing must be made by the beneficiaries under the terms of the will at the date of death.
2. This written notification must be made within two years after the person's death.
3. The deed of variation must clearly set out the altered parts of the will and the new destination of the property.
4. Written notice must be given to the Inland Revenue, otherwise it will not count as a transfer upon death for tax purposes.

Another example of the usefulness of a deed of variation is if your estate had gone to your surviving spouse (*note*, no tax is payable upon transfer between husband and wife), then the first £234,000 (provided the spouse also lives in the UK) could be diverted to another member of your family, upon all concerned agreeing to this, and still not incur any inheritance tax. In large estates, a deed of family arrangement could also include gifts to charities, which, as noted previously, are free from inheritance tax.

But suppose you die without making a will? Even if a person has died intestate, provided the main beneficiary, ie the surviving spouse or children, agrees, a deed of variation can be entered into.

Before deciding to take this step and going to a solicitor, the main beneficiaries should first consult a tax expert and ascertain how much tax could be saved. If the amount is small, then the fees for rearranging affairs might be as much as the tax payable.

This deed of variation is a very useful tax planning tool, and no doubt this Chancellor may look to amend it in due course.

Business property relief

Other tax reliefs that can be used include business property relief. This not only includes a business or part of it but also shares in certain companies. However, it excludes those in property or investment companies. This relief comes in the form of a discount in the value of the assets. The business property relief at 100 per cent has been extended to all holdings of shares in qualifying unquoted companies where death occurred after 6 April 1996 (previously only shareholdings in excess of 25 per cent qualified).

1. A sole proprietor's interest in the business is eligible for 100 per cent relief; a partner's interest also qualifies for 100 per cent relief.
2. Business relief at 100 per cent is also available in respect of controlling interest in a company, including that in an unquoted company.
3. One hundred per cent business relief is available for shareholdings in qualifying unquoted trading companies. Shares dealt with on the Unlisted Securities Market (USM) are not regarded as quoted shares.

   In cases where a controlling shareholder transfers assets that were used by the company but owned by the individual only 50 per cent relief is given.
4. For quoted companies valued on a controlling basis, ie a shareholding in excess of 50 per cent, the relief is 50 per cent.

Provided the recipient still owns the property – which must still be in use as a business and as such can genuinely be termed 'business property' – even if the gift falls into tax charge following your death within the seven years, it will still qualify for business property relief.

In addition, where a death occurred after 31 August 1995, there have been improvements made to the 100 per cent agricultural property relief relating to farmland that is subject to an agricultural tenancy that had been acquired following the death of the previous tenant. Importantly, any doubt concerning the transfer of value after Budget Day of 27 November 1995 of qualifying business or agricultural assets made within the seven years before death has been removed.

Relief for successful charges

Where one deceased person has inherited assets and in turn leaves those assets to another person who themselves die within five years, if the first person's estate has already paid inheritance tax, then should the second person's estate also attract inheritance tax, a reduction can be claimed. This is based on the following:

Table 6.5

Period between deaths	% reduction
< 1 year	100
1–2 years	80
2–3 years	60
3–4 years	40
4–5 years	20

To claim this, please ensure that you follow the instructions laid out in the inheritance tax guide with regard to successive charges.

Related property rules

The value of any shares held in a company can be increased because of what is known as the 'related property' rules. Under these rules your holding is combined with another and the appropriate portion of the value of the combined holding is taken against the value for inheritance tax purposes. For example, if you owned 35 per cent of the shares in your family's unquoted trading company and your spouse held another 35 per cent, bringing the total value held by you both to 70 per cent, this would give you full control of the business and much more than a minority holding of a single 35 per cent. What it would mean is that your shares would be valued at 50 per cent of the joint holding of 70 per cent.

Ignoring business property relief, because inheritance tax is payable on death based on the full asset value, in order to plan effectively you should not wait until the family firm has become successful before transferring shares to younger members of the family. Instead, you should transfer the shares to your children before the value increases. The best time to do this is when the company is first formed.

Although chargeable transfers have to be reported to the Inland Revenue within 12 months of a person's death, interest on late payment of inheritance tax starts to be charged as follows. For deaths occurring between 6 April and 30 September in any year, interest becomes payable from 30 April in the following year. For deaths that have taken place between 1 October and 5 April the following year, interest becomes payable six months after the end of the month in which death occurred; in other words if death happened on 29 October 1999, provided inheritance tax was applicable, interest would be charged from 1 May 2000.

In the 1999 Budget, increased penalties were announced with regard to the late or non-payment of inheritence tax. These are:

1. If those liable for inheritence tax or the dead person's representatives do not submit a full account within 12 months of death to the Revenue, a fine of £100 is charged.
2. Giving fraudulent information on this form now incurs a penalty of £3,000 plus extra tax.
3. Incorrect information, ie negligence, by the personal representative attracts a penalty of £1,000.
4. Finally, fraudulent information attracts a fine of £3,000 against the personal representative(s).

The tax payable on any land or business assets which Great Uncle Harry may have owned, including controlling shares, may be paid over 10 years, interest free. It sometimes happens that shares are sold within 12 months of a person's death for less than the stated probate value. The person liable to inheritance tax can claim that the sale price be substituted for the original probate value provided that the proceeds are not later reinvested into that same company.

Suppose that you were selling Great Uncle Harry's shares, the probate value being £7,000, and because of a fall in the stock market you have only managed to obtain £5,000; if you are liable to the inheritance tax on his estate, you can claim back the original probate value less the sale price, provided that the proceeds are not then reinvested into the same company.

A similar rule applies to land. If land is sold for less than the probate value within a three-year period, the sale price can be substituted for the probate price. If Great Uncle Harry had received money from someone else's estate on which he had paid inheritance tax, provided it had occurred over the last five years the following deduction of the original tax is given:

Table 6.6

	%
0–1 years	100
1–2 years	80
2–3 years	60
3–4 years	40
4–5 years	20

Disposing of an asset

If you, as a donor, dispose of an asset to another person but retain an interest in that asset, for inheritance tax purposes it is not seen as being an effective transfer as it has a 'prior reservation'. Under the old capital taxes rules a popular method of tax planning used to be for a couple to give shares in their main residence to their children as tenants-in-common which they then continue to occupy. This transfer substantially reduced the value of the estate. With the introduction of reservation rules it was first thought that this method would be ineffective as the donors would continue to occupy the whole of the house, including the gifted share. However, during the Finance Bill 1986 a government spokesman went on record to state that the reservation rules would not apply in the following circumstances:

Elderly parents make unconditional gifts of individual shares of their house to their children and the parents and the children continue to occupy the property as the family home, such owner bearing his or her running costs. In those circumstances it is thought that the donors' occupation is termed as one for full consideration whereby, because each has a use of each other's part of the house and each bears the cost of maintenance then the reservation rules can be set aside.

In many circumstances, however, it would not be practical for the beneficiaries also to reside in the property, so this line of tax planning has, within certain limitations, now been blocked, unless the former owners pay a commercial rent for the property afterwards.

As trusts can be useful tax-planning vehicles with regard to inheritance tax, it is worthwhile considering the different types of trusts and how effective they can be in inheritance tax planning. However, if you are going to set up a trust, then you must go to a solicitor and ask for his or her assistance.

Interest in possession trusts

Although not defined in the tax legislation, an 'interest in possession' exists when someone is absolutely entitled to the trust's income. When that interest comes to an end because of the life tenant's death, the assets of the trust are added together with the person's free estate (in other words, whatever is owned outside the life tenancy) to determine the total amount of inheritance tax payable by the tenant's estate. The trustees will become liable to tax on a pro-rata share of the total tax payable. If you dispose of your interest during your lifetime, the value of the trust is treated by the tax authorities as a lifetime gift and would be taxed according to the lifetime tax rates applicable to yourself. This means that if your tax rate is 40 per cent, then whatever assets are yours and incur inheritance tax will also be taxed at 40 per cent.

There are three occasions when no inheritance tax will be payable, and these are:

1. Where you have the interest in possession and become absolutely entitled to the assets of the trust.
2. Where the property of that trust reverts to the settlor's spouse (the *settlor* is the person who has made the trust out)

during the settlement lifetime or, if death occurs, within a two-year period.
3. Where the life tenant is the surviving widow or widower of the settlement and the old estate duty (pre-1974) was paid when the spouse died.

Children: accumulation and maintenance settlements

This type of settlement is an extension of a discretionary settlement with inheritance tax advantages provided the following criteria can be satisfied:

1. At least one of the beneficiaries will become entitled to at least the income from the trust if not the capital at the age of 25.
2. The income in the meantime must be accumulated or applied towards the education of the child or children.
3. No more than 25 years can elapse since the settlement was first made and all the beneficiaries are the grandchildren of common grandparents. In such a case there is no tax payable when setting up the trust (assuming that the donor survives for a period of seven years), although there is a 10-year anniversary charge.

If you are a 40 per cent taxpayer and your estate is likely to be well over the inheritance tax threshold, assuming you have grandchildren, it is worthwhile to commence a trust for their benefit. The trust rate of tax is higher than most at 34 per cent, but where sums have been paid out to the child(ren) and where these sums have had tax paid, then the child(ren)'s parents/guardians can reclaim the tax deducted, assuming that the child(ren)'s personal allowance has not been exceeded.

Most people are pleasantly surprised when working out the valuation of their estate. How to value an estate is explained in Chapter 10. It is important to have an overall value of your estate in order to minimise the tax liabilities which your estate or beneficiaries will face.

By planning in advance, for example, by equalising the estate and the income produced by it, you can ensure that your estate – and your family's affairs – are in a more tax-efficient position. Equalising assets also has an added benefit in that in 1990 a new tax treatment was introduced for wives.

Discretionary trusts

With a discretionary settlement no one has an interest in possession as seen by the tax authority and inheritance tax is payable in the following circumstances:

1. When capital is first put into the settlement.
2. When capital is distributed to the beneficiary or beneficiaries.
3. On the tenth anniversary of the settlement, tax is payable on 15 per cent of the death rate.

It is not within the capacity of this book to deal comprehensively with trusts as an entity as they are a personal financial tax vehicle to each individual's estate and should be individually planned. If you wish to draw up a trust, then you should go to a solicitor as well as a tax consultant for assistance. However, as a tax vehicle, a two-year discretionary trust will be briefly discussed.

This is a very flexible type of trust and can be used, for example, if you wish your estate to be held in trust for your spouse and/or children for a period of two years from your death. During that time capital from the trust can be paid out to trust members at the executor's discretion. It means that your spouse and children can get money when they most need it without incurring a heavy tax burden. The decision as to who needs what and when allows the trust's executor to distribute the estate as tax-efficiently as possible.

Jointly owned property

Property can be owned in two ways. The first is in a joint tenancy and the second is in a tenancy-in-common. In a joint tenancy, when the co-owner dies the surviving co-owner automatically takes over the deceased's half irrespective of provisions in his or her will. Of course, a solicitor should have been used to adjust the property's title deeds to this effect.

Tenancy-in-common means that the deceased's share of the house passes to the estate under the terms of the will. From a tax point of view, whether the husband inherits his share from his wife or *vice versa*, if the property is jointly owned by them then the share will be exempt from inheritance tax under the 'surviving spouse' exemption. If the property is owned jointly by two friends or, say, by a mother and son, the share will become liable to inheritance tax as it is not applicable under the above-stated exemption.

If a mother wanted her son eventually to inherit her half of the house (held as tenants-in-common), she could write in her will that a life interest goes to her husband but that on his death her son receives her share. By doing this she ensures that her son eventually inherits her half. If, for example, she were a co-owner in a joint tenancy, after her death it would pass automatically to the husband, and if he remarried, his new wife would become entitled to the whole of the house upon the father's death unless he made a will to the contrary. This could not happen under a tenancy-in-common as the husband and the new wife would live in the house but on the husband's death his first wife's share in the property would pass to her son.

How is tax paid?

Inheritance tax forms have recently been changed and they are now far easier to follow and complete than before. The Guides have also been written in a more readable and understandable way. When you contact either the order line (0845 900 0404) or the Capital Taxes offices, these will be sent out to you. Form IHT 200, for example, has IHT 210 as guide notes. Supplementary pages SP1 and SP2, which accompany the supplementary pages, break down the various assets into manageable portions, such as shares, property, pensions, etc.

When the executor or administrator has completed the Inland Revenue forms received from and returned to the Probate Registry (or in Scotland from the Commissary Office), the Registry will, if it is appropriate, send the forms to the Capital Taxes Office at Ferrers House, PO Box 38, Castle Meadow Road, Nottingham NG2 1BB (Tel: 0115 974 2400) or to the Belfast office, Level 3, Dorchester House, 52–58 Great Victoria Street, Belfast BT2 7QL. Here the information contained in the forms will be assessed to see whether or not any tax is immediately payable. Tax due on an estate other than a house, property or land or share in a private company must be paid before the grant of probate or letters of administration are issued.

Usually, the executor is informed by the Probate Registry – on behalf of the Inland Revenue – if any tax is due and the amount. If the assessment is incorrect or you cannot agree with this assessment, you should write immediately to the tax authorities stating the reason why you do not agree with their assessment. If the grant has not as yet been issued by the Probate Registry, then you should write to them in the first instance. Always quote the reference number given on any replies received from the authorities. If dealing with the Inland Revenue direct, then you should note all the details of the will, for example, the deceased's name, address, the date probate was granted and what Probate Registry was dealing with matters.

As can be imagined, a difficulty arises when the testator has not taken into account the value of the estate grossed up. For example, say you left £260,000 outright and had distributed this same amount under the terms of your will, making no allowance for tax to be deducted from your estate. Your beneficiaries or the residuary beneficiary would only receive a portion of your written declaration because tax would first have to be paid before probate and distribution took place (ie £260,000 – £234,000 = £26,000 × 40% = £10,400, ∴ distribution = £249,600). So a word of warning, inheritance tax can damage your wealth!

To make these calculations simpler, the Revenue has produced tax tables showing what inheritance tax is due on different amounts of grossed up estates. Once you have valued your estate it may be worthwhile to ask your local HM Inspector of Taxes' office to forward a copy to you so that you can make sure that your calculations are correct. (See page 69 for the table on how to calculate inheritance tax.)

Always remember that the Revenue works on the principle that the tax payable on the legacy is an integral part of your estate and in most cases must be paid before distribution can take place.

Any tax that needs to be paid across to the tax authority needs to be deducted from income and not from capital. The author knows of a particular case where a solicitor who was the executor/trustee had tax deducted from capital not income, thus favouring the life tenant, who was also his personal client.

Insurance against inheritance tax

You can insure your estate against paying inheritance tax but be warned, it is expensive. Basically, the insurance companies work on the principle that the older you are the higher the premiums become as the day of your 'parting' is that much closer.

It could be argued that, for the increased premiums asked, if the same amount were put aside and invested then this extra money could achieve much the same end in alleviating the tax burden when it falls, as long as you take into account what you need to earn and set aside for inheritance tax. Of course, the best 'insurance policy' is to make sure that you have already taken all necessary estate planning measures.

7

Dealing With Personal Tax Matters After Death

The administrator, shortly after the death of an individual who has died without making a will, has to settle the deceased's personal tax liabilities. He has to see that any income tax, capital gains tax or inheritance tax liabilities are paid to the Inland Revenue. Handling these affairs can not only mean paying out money to clear the tax bill but also applying for a refund of tax from the Inspector of Taxes. Whichever applies, the amounts are seen as either a liability or an asset of the deceased person's estate as at the date of death, and will affect the amount of inheritance tax due.

In April 1996 a new system of tax collection was introduced, known as self-assessment. For further information please see page 92. The idea behind this change was that the onus to pay tax falls on the taxpayer (executor or trustee) as it has always done but that the *taxpayer* has to advise the Revenue of this. Penalties are much higher than before.

As executor, you should be aware that there are a number of time limitations set by the tax authority for raising an assessment for tax on the deceased's estate.

1. Under Section 40(1) Taxes Management Act 1970, the Inland Revenue must raise the assessment within three years of the end of the tax year in which the death took place. In other words, if a person died on 1 March 1997, then the assessment must be raised by the Revenue no later than 5 April 2000.

2. Under Section 34(1) Taxes Management Act 1970, any assessment raised within the three-year period mentioned

in 1. can only relate to the deceased person's six previous taxable years. In other words, if a person died on 6 January 1995 (this would fall within the 1994/95 tax year), the Revenue could raise a tax assessment(s) for any (or all) of the previous six years prior to his death.

3. If the Inland Revenue can show that tax has been lost to the Crown by 'wilful default or fraud', the Inland Revenue may raise an assessment on the executor within the previously stated three years relating to any tax year. (A tax year is seen as 12 full months running from 6 April in the first year to 5 April in the following year.) The Revenue's assessment starts with the three years and ends within the six years from the date of death.

In the income tax year in which the death took place, the deceased person will be assessed for tax under various schedules right up to the date of death. There is no apportionment of income in income tax law. For example, income from property assessed under income tax schedule A is assessed on rents due to the deceased prior to the date of death regardless of whether the money has been received before or after the date of death. The normal cessation rules apply. In other words, income is assessable to income tax schedule D, cases I to V, and any amounts that are received under the deduction of basic rate tax, eg dividend income from shares, will only form part of the deceased person's income if the payment date shown on the dividend voucher falls before the date of death.

However, it does not matter if the payment date on the dividend voucher falls after the date of death. In this instance, the payment becomes income received during the period of administration and therefore there is no question of time apportionment. This makes life somewhat simpler as there is, in general executorship law, the assessment of income tax in the year of death, and this is a relatively simple matter.

Allowable expenses before inheritance tax

The following are the most common deductions made from the gross value of an estate in order to arrive at a figure of net value before the inheritance tax is calculated.

1. Certain exempt transfers such as donations to registered charities, political parties with two or more elected MPs, etc.
2. Funeral expenses.
3. Debts owed at the date of death payable in the UK, although certain gifts after the March 1986 Budget can be disallowed if you made connected gifts to those creditors or the debt was not wholly for your own consideration.
4. Legal and professional fees owing up to the date of death.
5. Income tax and capital gains tax liabilities up to the time of death whether or not an assessment has been raised at that time.

No allowance against inheritance tax can be made for either probate expenses or executors' expenses.

Any debts arising outside the UK are normally deducted only from assets that are themselves situated outside the UK.

How does this affect the surviving partner's tax position?

Following the Chancellor's 1999 Budget, both widows and widowers receive a rather raw deal from 6 April 2000. The widow's bereavement allowance has been cut. This means that a widow who previously would have had a direct reduction in tax of £570 (ie current allowance of £1,900 × 2 years × 15 per cent) will lose it. A double blow at a time when the state earnings pension scheme payments for bereaved spouses will be halved. Only the bereavement payment proposed in the Welfare Reform and Pensions Act is allowed but sadly only to those under 60. Fortunately, both sexes will be able to claim it.

Husband

The married couple's allowance is no longer deducted from total income. Indeed, from 6 April 2000 it has been phased out totally except in cases where one partner was over 65 before 6 April 2000. In these cases the age-related married couples allowance is still given. This is for 2000/01 £5,185 at 10 per cent. It increases in amount for those over 75 in tax year 2000/01 to £5,225 at 10 per cent. However, from 6 April 1995 to 5 April 1999 there was a restriction of 15p in £1 and from

April 1999 this was further reduced to 10 per cent. This equals the sum of £285.00 (1998/99) that can be deducted from a person's net tax liability (ie allowance £1,900 × 15%). The same now applies to the widow's bereavement allowance. The basic personal allowance for 1999/00 is £4,335 and for 2000/01 £4,385. Since 6 April 2000 there is no widow's bereavement allowance nor is there an additional personal allowance.

A widow's income may include that from her late husband's estate. This is dealt with in more detail later in this chapter.

Wife

Following the introduction of the independant taxation of a wife's income, the single person's allowance applies, as noted above. All other allowances previously available have been abolished.

Since 6 April 1999 the tax on building society interest has been reduced to 20 per cent in line with the tax percentage on dividends. However, as of 6 April 1999 the start rate of tax had been reduced to 10 per cent on the first £1,500 of income; if you are in a repayment tax situation you can claim the difference on a repayment form.

If a person is over the age of 65 and his or her income does not exceed £16,800 (1999/00), then that person will be eligible for higher personal age allowance. This increases again when a person is over the age of 75.

Any investment income arising from assets held, such as stocks and shares, will be taxed in the hands of a wife's executor and ultimately form part of her husband's income to the extent that he is the ultimate beneficiary.

The Inland Revenue has now produced a helpful leaflet entitled '*What Happens when Someone Dies?*' (IR 45), which can be obtained from any Inland Revenue Office.

Self-assessment

From 6 April 1996 a new tax system was phased in, called self-assessment. From this date, it became a legal responsibility of each individual (whether or not in business or employed or retired) to keep full and proper records for both income tax purposes and capital gains. These records must be retained by individuals for 24 months after the end of the tax year in which they relate, 22 months after the end of the tax year in which they relate for executors, and five years for business.

The new system removes the onus from the Inland Revenue to calculate tax due and firmly places this on the individual. Failure to keep accurate records or late submission of your return and monies due will result in stiff financial penalties.

If individuals or businesses wish to submit their returns and calculations, then these must be with the Revenue no later than 31 January after the end of the tax year or, if later, three months after issue of the return. A self-assessment of your tax liabilities must also accompany your return. The Revenue will do the calculations for you but they must receive all your records by 30 September after the end of the tax year or two months after the date of issue of the return.

As an executor, self-assessment obliges you to keep complete and accurate records and to continue to keep the records of the testator. You will have to complete, as you do now, a return up until the date of death, and one for the period of administration.

If there is more than one executor of a will or trustee of a trust, then each individual is liable to complete a return. In this instance it is best for the executors/trustees to select one of their number, who is familiar with the return, to do this. Returns, following self-assessment, have changed in their appearance. If no executor or trustee feels able to complete the return, then a tax adviser should be sought. Payment for his or her fees are set off against any income that is earned, even if the income is paid direct to the life tenant by the will.

The Capital Taxes Office send out a guide with the Tax Return. It sets out how the calculation is worked out, what expenses are deductible and so on.

If returns are late in their submission to the Revenue, then the Revenue have the power to issue a penalty of £100, which itself is interest-bearing. The only way out of this is to submit your self-assessment return.

Where a settlement under a trust exists, and there is more than one trustee, each trustee will need to make a return and be accountable for errors and omissions in both income tax and capital gains tax.

Penalties have been increased for people who do not pay inheritance tax, see below for details.

What is a tax code?

The tax allowances that are given to you are shown in the income tax coding sent to you by the Inland Revenue. If you have any doubts as to its correctness, then telephone the Revenue, reiterating your circumstances and the income earned and ask for your code to be checked.

The income tax code shows figures and a letter. The figures indicate the amount you are allowed to earn before tax and the letter states what category you are in.

Any change in your circumstances should be notified to the Revenue so that your code can be adjusted.

Income tax due during the period of administration

Wherever you live in the United Kingdom, any tax matters mentioned in this book will apply as the Inland Revenue – unlike the Probate Registry or Commissary Office – covers the whole of the United Kingdom, except for the Channel Islands and the Isle of Man.

An executor's duties start after a person's death. Often the responsibility for making the funeral arrangements falls on the executor. Your duties as executor continue throughout the period of administration, collecting the assets, paying the creditors, seeing that specific legacies are paid off and the residuary legatee (the person whom the remainder of the estate goes to) is informed of the balance.

In your final correspondence a letter should be sent to the residuary beneficiary in which you list all the remaining assets available. By doing this the residue is then stated to have been 'ascertained'.

When you consent to the beneficiary taking these assets over it is termed as 'assenting to the residuary bequest'. At the same time as you send this letter you should also send a copy of the estate's accounts and ask the beneficiary to sign them as proof of the formal discharge. When this is done you have effectively ended the period of administration.

It may be that under the terms of the will the deceased created a trust. At this point you, as the executor, cease to be the executor and become the trustee.

From the date of death the executor receives all income which arises from any of the deceased person's estate, some of which will be taxed at source. In other words, the sending organisation will already have deducted tax (unless an account holder is not liable to tax and has signed an appropriate form from the bank or building society). This usually happens with building society or bank accounts; dividends gained from company shares would have had 10 per cent tax deducted at source if the deceased was liable to tax. Additional tax may have to be paid if the deceased's income was over the relevant threshold. Other income, such as rental from property and so on, is untaxed and is sent directly to the executor. The Inland Revenue will raise an assessment on you in your role as executor of the estate. This does not mean that your own personal tax affairs are affected.

Although as the executor you are not entitled to claim for a personal allowance on the deceased's behalf, you are entitled to claim for losses made after the person's death while you are running his or her business. As far as the income tax rules are concerned, the death of a trader and the subsequent passing of his or her business to a successor normally marks the end or cessation of a trade.

As an executor you can also obtain income tax relief for the estate on interest payments, if those interest payments would have been deducted for tax purposes for the deceased. As an executor you may also have to obtain a loan, using the estate as security, so that the inheritance tax bill can be met. It should be noted that the personal representatives of the deceased can obtain income tax relief on interest paid on a loan within a one-year period of raising that loan, provided it was used to pay for inheritance tax. If the interest cannot be relieved wholly in the year when it is paid, it can either be carried back or forward as required. As an executor, you are never assessed to the higher rates of income tax during the period of administration.

If you continue to run the deceased's business, then the profits made become liable to income tax under schedule D, case I or II. If you merely sell off trading stock, there would be no income tax liability whatsoever.

Expenses incurred while administering the estate are not allowable for income tax and must be met from taxed income. Interest on non-payment of inheritance tax (which runs from six months after the end of the month in which the death occurred) is also not considered to be an expense and is therefore not allowable to be set against income tax. Executor's expenses are not considered to be tax deductible, including solicitors' charges.

As seen earlier, dividend income received after the date of death forms part of the income of the estate as it was received during the period of administration. This is so even if the accounting year in which it was declared may have fallen before the date of death. All income received during the period of administration is liable to basic rate income tax, which is 22 per cent from 6 April 2000 and 10p in £1 starting rate on the first £1,520.

If a beneficiary is not liable to income tax because the income is covered by the existing personal allowance, the income tax deducted by you as the executor can be reclaimed. If the beneficiary is in the higher rate of income tax, currently 40 per cent, he or she will have to pay additional income tax.

The distribution of income to a beneficiary

As an executor you should be aware of the implications of distribution of income to the beneficiary. The amount of income to which a legatee becomes entitled depends on the terms of his or her legacy.

General legacies

A specific sum of money, say, £5,000 or an asset, say, 'my motor car' is referred to as capital matter. As capital matter it means that the person inheriting it is not entitled to any income during the period of administration unless the will directs that interest is to be paid on the legacy. If this is so, then the beneficiary is liable to income tax under schedule D, case III on the amount received. This can prove to be expensive from the tax point of view as the estate income has already been taxed once at the basic rate of tax.

Once the money has been paid out to the beneficiary, the interest paid out by you on the net amount becomes liable to tax as though it were a gross receipt. This harsh tax treatment also applies to the interest payable to the surviving spouse in intestacy cases (for fuller details of tax applicable in intestacy cases see section 46 of the Administration of Estates Act 1925).

Specific legacies
This term refers to a gift of, say, £10,000 of 13 per cent Treasury Stock 2000, and entitles the beneficiary to the interest incurred on a day-to-day basis from the date of death. Any interest received prior to the person's death forms part of the residue of the estate.

Annuities
This may be a gift of, say, £1,000 stipulated in the will to be paid over a specified period of time, say 20 years from the date of death. On each anniversary of that person's death you, as the executor, would have to distribute £1,000 less tax of 22 per cent. The beneficiary would receive £780. As it is paid out of income that has already been taxed at the basic rate of tax, the real cost to the estate is only £780. This is in sharp contrast to the general legacy which would have been taxed twice.

The residue of the estate
The main beneficiary under the terms of the will is entitled to the remainder of the estate and is also entitled to any income received unless it is left in trust. If this is the case, then the life tenancy of the residue of the estate is only entitled to the income arising after the person's death.

The death of a life tenant does not result in any capital gains tax becoming payable, even if the assets are chargeable ones and have increased in value since the original death.

The tax position in the case of the residue of the estate being given absolutely to the beneficiary is as follows. The residuary income of the estate is the total income *less* the interest and expenses relating to that income. The total income less tax, at the basic rate, and interest and expenses is then grossed up and forms part of the beneficiary's total income. Each year, you would have to supply the beneficiary with a certificate of tax deduction (form R185) which he or she can then use to claim back the deducted tax if applicable.

Where a person has only a life interest in the estate, the tax position is different. The net income for the whole of the administration period, less the interest and expenses, etc, is seen to have accrued evenly over the period and the amount is allocated to each tax year and is grossed up to the basic rate of tax for the year applicable. These rates are:

2000/01	22 per cent
1999/00	22 per cent
1998/99	23 per cent
1997/98	23 per cent
1996/97	24 per cent
1995/96	25 per cent
1994/95	25 per cent
1993/94	25 per cent
1992/93	25 per cent
1991/92	25 per cent
1990/91	25 per cent
1989/90	25 per cent
1988/89	25 per cent

Under this rule the amounts may have been taxed on the executor at one rate of basic tax but grossed up on the beneficiary at another rate. Therefore, it would be best, if possible, to distribute the estate within a 12-month period after the date of death and avoid letting proceedings be drawn out for subsequent years.

8

Who Can You Go To For Help?

Some executors would not consider administering an estate without the help of a solicitor. There might be a number of reasons why, such as complexities arising from property within an estate or the existence of a trust. More to the point, however, an executor might not be able to dedicate the number of man-hours necessary to the task of administering an estate. And, of course, personal grief might play an important role when perhaps the executor feels emotionally unable to cope.

If a personal application is to be made but you wish to be excused from acting as executor, you must send a letter to the Probate Registry explaining that you feel you are unable to continue and request that you be discharged from your duties. The Registry will then prepare a formal document known as a *letter of renunciation* for you to sign. This document must also be witnessed. If you are dealing through a solicitor, the renunciation will be prepared for you. Should the will be in your possession, and you wish to renounce your involvement but do not know any relatives or beneficiaries of the will and therefore cannot hand it over to them for their own application, you can hand it over to your nearest Probate Registry along with your renunciation. A formal receipt will be given for the documents.

When will you need assistance?

The following is a list of foreseeable complications that might necessitate an inexperienced executor applying for professional advice, whether it is for the entire duty or only part of it.

1. If the deceased owned a business or was a partner in a business.
2. Family trusts or life interest.
3. If there are any persons benefiting from the estate who are under the age of 18.
4. Loss of will.
5. The possibility of a distant relative claiming inheritance and possible court action thereafter.
6. An inadequately worded will.
7. Insolvency of the estate.
8. If a property that forms part of the estate has an unregistered title.
9. The possibility that unknown debts may arise.

Most of these points are concerned with the distribution of the estate. Before you require help you can start proceedings yourself and speed up the actual obtaining of the grant of probate or letters of administration. This application is a simple matter and then later, if the affairs begin to look complicated, or lack of time or whatever reason prevents you from continuing, you can seek further advice from a financial adviser, tax consultant or solicitor, whichever profession is appropriate to your needs.

Occasionally, situations arise where it is not considered appropriate for you to obtain a grant through the Personal Applications Department of the Probate Registry. However, it is extremely rare for an application to be refused, as 999 out of 1,000 are accepted.

Where do you start?

If in doubt about any matters regarding probate, contact the Personal Applications Department of the Probate Registry and talk to the staff at the nearest Registry to you. They are in the best position to advise whether the application may be accepted or whether it would be best to instruct a solicitor. It should be remembered that even solicitors' applications are eventually sent to the Probate Registry for completion, so the staff there are competent to give you advice on most aspects of the procedures. However, they are not allowed to give actual legal advice outside their field.

Solicitors

When making out a will, if you are self-employed or a partner in a business, or if there is substantial property involved, you will need to use the services of a solicitor. For example, in a partnership between yourself and another person (or group of people) a document called a *partnership agreement* would need to be drawn up. This would stipulate all business arrangements agreed between you and your partner(s) and state what is to happen when any one of the partners leaves the business or dies. This agreement needs to be drawn up before you go into business and reference to it needs to be made in your will.

A solicitor's help would also be necessary if you wanted a trust to be drawn up or if you were in an insurance syndicate. In such cases the estate is likely to be complicated and you will definitely need help to pull all the matters together to make them more manageable to administer after your death.

In the case of intestacy, as an administrator you might need a solicitor if complications arise, such as difficulties in tracing missing relatives or living relatives residing overseas. This problem is a fairly common one and solicitors know the many ways to have relatives traced.

Solicitors will, if you wish, also keep your will on their premises if they have drawn it up for you or if you are a regular client.

The benefit of using solicitors as opposed to other professional advisers is that their 'watchdog', the Law Society, keeps an eye on solicitors' actions. For example, if you consider that you have been overcharged, you can write asking for its opinion and, if the Law Society is in agreement with you, seek a rebate.

Solicitors charge for drawing up a will and this cost can range upwards from £50 per will, depending upon complexities within the estate and the time that has to be spent. Be aware, however, that some firms of solicitors charge say £50 plus VAT for writing a will when in effect it would have cost them in time spent upward of £150 plus VAT. If they are named as executors, it is worth noting what their charges are, as you may find these could be £120 per hour or more, well in excess of the charge for making the will. Taking this example further, using a solicitor to handle probate on an average estate could well cost you in excess of £2,500 plus VAT if not more, and that is with close monitoring of costs. If the solicitor does not give you written details of charge rates when you first become his or her client, then he or she is in breach of one of the rules of the Law Society's Code of Conduct. Naturally, you have to be realistic when judging how much the bills should be; like everyone else, solicitors have to earn a crust!

The more complicated and lengthy a will is, the higher the charge for the will should be. A word of advice; if your will is likely to be complicated or there are any unusual circumstances, go to a solicitor for help. In order to save time and cost, before meeting your solicitor note down in detail your anticipated plans for division of your estate.

Incidentally, the Law Society now sells a document called a 'Personal Assets Log', which can be used to list the location of all your important papers, whether they are your will or the deed to your property. Whether or not you decide to use the log, it is a good idea to make known to your immediate family the location of all relevant documents.

Another instance where you could benefit from professional advice is in the case of intestacy if the estate is valued at over £125,000 where there are children or issue. By current law, the surviving spouse inherits a life interest in half of the property over that figure of £125,000 and the children receive the other half.

Ambiguity in the meaning or irregularity in the terms of the will may give rise to other instances where professional advice is needed. But again, this need not stop you from initially taking the grant of probate as a personal applicant.

If a person died with debts exceeding assets, despite a will having been made, the estate is insolvent and the beneficiaries would not be able to receive any legacies. In this instance, as executor it would be sensible to employ a professional adviser to unravel the case, because creditors are paid in a strict order of priority in accordance with bankruptcy laws. The cost of these expenses would be paid for from the estate even before any beneficiary or creditor. This particular problem can throw out complications which are many and varied, one being that claims submitted may exceed the known sum owed.

Another complication can be the possibility of someone making a claim against the estate, seeking to gain a share or a larger share or money that the deceased owed. Advice from your solicitor would be essential since either negotiations will need to take place to decide on the portion to be awarded (if the claimant does have a case) or because the claimant contesting the matter is taking the case to court.

These may all sound quite alarming but in the majority of cases matters are relatively straightforward with complexities rarely arising. Simple problems can be dealt with by asking the staff at the Personal Applications Department at the Probate Registry what the best course of action would be or whom you should go to.

The Probate Registry

The Probate Registry is part of the Family Division within the High Court structure and as such comes within the Civil Court responsible to the Lord Chancellor's office. The Registry dates back to Norman times when Bishops Courts began to administer the wills of the deceased.

In 1357, the Courts were required by statute to pass on the administration of property from the Bishops Courts to the deceased's closest relative. In 1857, a further change took place when the District Probate Registries were introduced as a division within the Probate, Admiralty and Divorce Division of the High Court. In 1970 the Administration of Justice Act placed the probate section in the newly founded Family Division within the High Court, where it remains today.

The Probate Registry in England and Wales is unusual in that it provides people with advice and assistance that may be needed in order for them, as individuals, to obtain the grant of probate or letters of administration. In Scotland, the Commissary Court does give assistance but this is limited to small estates.

How can it help?
The Probate Registry is the linchpin of the proceedings. Its equivalent in Scotland is the Commissary Office.

The main function of the Registry is to give a grant of representation to the executor or next of kin. This grant is a document bearing the court seal, which states that the person named is authorised to deal with the estate. In fact, the document empowers that person to do anything that the deceased could have done if he or she were alive.

The Registry cannot advise you on making a will. It can, however, deal with any queries you may have in connection with making the will.

Probate Registries and Probate Sub-Registries are open daily during normal office hours. The probate administration system in England and Wales is a three-tiered one. There are 11 District Probate Registries in England and Wales and, of course, there is also Somerset House. The Registries also have Sub-Registries linked to them. There are also small Probate Offices which deal only with personal callers. These offices may be open for only one day a week or, in some cases, one day a month. Local Probate Offices are linked not only to Registries but to Sub-Registries as well. You will be asked which office is most convenient for you to attend.

All branches send out application forms, which start the whole proceedings, from their Personal Applications Department. Proceedings are straightforward. There is a list of Registries, Sub-Registries and Offices on pages 105–08.

Upon telephoning or writing to the Registry you will receive an envelope containing all the forms that are needed. The turn-round time for dealing with these is usually two or three weeks, although proceedings can be speeded up. The delay is not caused here but usually when the executor is trying to pull together all the details of the estate.

A probate fee is payable for estates over £5,000 at a flat rate of £130 for deaths after 26 April 1999. No fee is charged for estates under £5,000. See Appendix 2 on page 159 for charges before 26 April 1999.

Once probate has been granted, executors can proceed to collect in and transfer monies to debtors and beneficiaries.

When neither a will nor a relative can be found the probate Treasury Solicitor will take over the duties. The Treasury Solicitor will make enquiries on behalf of the Crown to trace relatives. After considerable checking to see whether there are any living relatives with valid claims he will then declare none has been found, and only then does the Crown become entitled to the estate. (It is possible that a dependant of the deceased may make a claim against the estate, for example, a common-law husband or wife, or close friends who helped the deceased over the years without payment, or creditors.)

There are three types of document issued by the Probate Registry, namely, Grant of Probate when there is a valid will with executors applying; Letters of Administration when there is a valid will but executors have not been appointed; or Letters of Administration given when there is no will.

There are three areas where Grant of Probate or Letters of Administration may not be needed.

1. If the property consists of cash (ie physical notes and coins), if the effects are household ones or a car, and provided there is no dispute between the immediate relatives as to the distribution.
2. If there is no more than £5,000 held in savings accounts or in National Savings and pension funds, it is possible that the sums may be released without the need for a grant. However, this is discretionary and the National Savings Bank may ask for a grant to be taken if it considers that circumstances require it.
3. Individual sums of money in banks and building societies do not exceed £5,000. However, many of the banks make a charge for preparing documents.

Probate Registries and their local Probate Offices

Bangor – Probate Sub-registry, Council Office, Ffordd, Gwynedd, Bangor LL57 1DT. Tel 01248 362410.
Local Probate Offices – Rhyl, Wrexham.
Birmingham – The Priory Courts, 33 Bull Street, Birmingham B4 6DU. Tel 0121 681 3400/3414.
Local Probate Offices – Coventry, Kidderminster, Lichfield, Northampton, Wolverhampton.
Bodmin – Market Street, Bodmin PL31 2JW. Tel 01208 72279.
Local Probate Offices – Penzance, Truro.

Brighton – William Street, Brighton BN2 2LG. Tel 01273 684071.
Local Probate Offices – Chichester, Crawley, Hastings.
Bristol – The Crescent Centre, Temple Back, Bristol BS1 6EP. Tel 0117 927 3915/927 4619.
Local Probate Offices – Bath, Weston-super-Mare.
Cardiff – Probate Registry of Wales, PO Box 474, 2 Park Street, Cardiff CF1 1TB. Tel 029 20376479.
Local Probate Offices – Bridgend, Newport, Pontypridd.
Carlisle – Courts of Justice, Earl Street, Carlisle CA1 1DJ. Tel 01228 21751.
Local Probate Office – Workington.
Carmarthen – 14 King Street, Carmarthen, Dyfed SA31 1BL. Tel 01267 236238.
Local Probate Offices – Aberystwyth, Haverfordwest, Swansea.
Chester – 5th Floor, Hamilton House, Hamilton Place, Chester CH1 2DA. Tel 01244 345082.
Exeter – Finance House, Barnfield Road, Exeter EX1 1QR. Tel 01392 274515.
Local Probate Offices – Barnstaple, Newton Abbot, Plymouth, Taunton, Yeovil.
Gloucester – 2nd Floor, Combined Court Building, Kimbrose Way, Gloucester GL1 2DG. Tel 01452 522585.
Local Probate Offices – Cheltenham, Hereford, Worcester.
Ipswich – Level 3, Haven House, 17 Lower Brook Street, Ipswich IP4 1DN. Tel 01473 253724/259261.
Local Probate Offices – Chelmsford, Colchester.
Lancaster – Mitre House, Church Street, Lancaster LA1 1HE. Tel 01524 36625.
Local Probate Offices – Barrow-in-Furness, Blackpool, Preston.
Leeds – 3rd Floor, Coronet House, Queen Street, Leeds LS1 2BA. Tel 0113 243 1505.
Local Probate Offices – Bradford, Harrogate, Huddersfield, Wakefield.
Leicester – 5th Floor, Leicester House, Lee Circle, Leicester LE1 3RE. Tel 0116 253 8558.
Local Probate Offices – Bedford, Kettering.
Lincoln – Mill House, Brayford Side North, Lincoln LN1 1YW. Tel 01522 523648.

Local Probate Office – Grimsby.
Liverpool – Queen Elizabeth II Law Courts, Derby Square, Liverpool L2 1XA. Tel 0151 236 8264.
Local Probate Offices – Southport, St Helens, Wallasey.
London – Probate Dept, Principal Registry Family Division, First Avenue House, 42–49 High Holborn, London WC1V 6NP. Tel 020 7936 6983.
Local Probate Offices – Croydon, Edmonton, Harlow, Kingston, Luton, Southend-on-Sea, Woolwich.
Maidstone – The Law Courts, Baker Road, Maidstone ME16 8EW. Tel 01622 202048.
Local Probate Offices – Canterbury, Chatham, Folkestone, Tunbridge Wells.
Manchester – 9th Floor, Astley House, 23 Quay Street, Manchester M3 4AT. Tel 0161 834 4319.
Local Probate Offices – Bolton, Nelson, Oldham, Stockport, Warrington, Wigan.
Middlesbrough – Combined Court Centre, Russell Street, Middlesbrough, Cleveland TS1 2AE. Tel 01642 340001.
Local Probate Offices – Darlington, Durham.
Newcastle-upon-Tyne – 2nd Floor, Plummer House, Croft Street, Newcastle-upon-Tyne NE1 6NP. Tel 0191 261 8383.
Local Probate Offices – Morpeth, Sunderland.
Norwich – Combined Court Building, The Law Courts, Bishopsgate, Norwich NR3 1UR. Tel 01603 761776.
Local Probate Office – Lowestoft.
Nottingham – Butt Dyke House, 33 Park Row, Nottingham NG1 6GR. Tel 0115 941 4288.
Local Probate Offices – Derby, Mansfield.
Oxford – 10A New Road, Oxford OX1 1LY. Tel 01865 241163.
Local Probate Offices – Aylesbury, High Wycombe, Reading, Slough, Swindon.
Peterborough – Crown Buildings, Rivergate, Peterborough PE1 1EJ. Tel 01733 62802.
Local Probate Offices – Cambridge, Kings Lynn.
Sheffield – PO Box 832, The Law Courts, 50 West Bar, Sheffield S3 8YR. Tel 0114 281 2596.
Local Probate Offices – Chesterfield, Doncaster.

Stoke-on-Trent – Combined Court Centre, Bethesda Street, Hanley, Stoke-on-Trent ST1 3BP. Tel 01782 854065.
Local Probate Offices – Crewe, Shrewsbury, Stafford.
Winchester – 4th Floor, Cromwell House, Andover Road, Winchester SO23 7EW. Tel 01962 863771.
Local Probate Offices – Basingstoke, Bournemouth, Dorchester, Guildford, Newport (Isle of Wight), Portsmouth, Salisbury, Southampton.
York – Duncombe Place, York YO1 2EA. Tel 01904 624210.
Local Probate Offices – Hull, Scarborough.

Where else can advice be sought?

The time to get in touch with your tax consultant should be before you start to make your will. Like the solicitor, the consultant will charge a fee for his or her time. But remember, not all accountants have estate planning experience and you need to check carefully that your chosen consultant does. Here again, ask how much the consultant charges per hour.

Your bank will also be able to offer help. Banks too charge a fee for dealing with probate matters and that charge can be steep, up to 5 per cent of the estate's value plus a withdrawal fee as well. Banks and solicitors also keep your will for safekeeping, or you may file it at your local Probate Registry or at Somerset House.

If it is necessary to have a bank account for the estate (known as an *executorship account*), remember to ask the bank what charge, if any, will be levied. Usually a bank charges a fee for administration – deducted from the account. But because of increased competition not only between banks but between building societies as well, charges and services are constantly changing. With some building societies now offering a banking service, it would be worthwhile shopping around for free banking.

Another organisation that can help is the Citizens' Advice Bureaux. This organisation has the advantage of having offices in all the major towns and cities throughout the United Kingdom. If one centre does not have the information, it can refer to a larger centre or recommend whom to go to.

When valuing the estate you may need to obtain valuations from different sources, depending on the estate's assets, and more importantly, the value in the estate. (If the estate is well under the inheritance tax threshold, then estimates from property valuers or jewellers will not be necessary.) For example, you may need to approach estate agents for property valuation, antique dealers for furniture, jewellers for jewellery and so on. Do ask if the valuation is free, otherwise you might find the estate faced with a bill. In addition to these 'property' valuations you will have to write to organisations such as banks and insurance companies, asking for a valuation of accounts or insurance policies. You might have to write to a publisher to ask for the current amount due on the royalties from a book; the list of contacts goes on, depending on the nature of the estate's assets.

THE "NOT FORGOTTEN" ASSOCIATION HELPS THE SERVING AND EX-SERVICE DISABLED FROM ALL CONFLICTS

There are almost 250,000 disabled ex-Service men and women in this country. They have been injured in conflicts from 1914 to the present day.

They all went to war knowing the risks, yet they accepted these courageously so that the rest of us could enjoy peace and freedom. Surely, we owe them a debt of honour for the sacrifices they made.

Now most of them are elderly and often frail. Their essential needs are provided for the State or other bodies. What we at The "Not Forgotten" Association do is to give them some of the "extras" which most of us take for granted – like television sets and licences, holidays, outings and entertainments. In short, something to look forward to. Please help us to make them feel that they matter – that they are not forgotten.

Call us on 020 7730 2400/3660 or fax us on 020 7730 0020 or visit our website at http://www.nfassociation.freeserve.co.uk
E-mail Director@infassociation.freeserve.co.uk

The "Not Forgotten" Association
4th Floor
2 Grosvenor Gardens
London SW1W 0DH
Patron: HRH The Duchess of Kent GCVO

Reg. Charity No 229666

9

Documentation

Death certificate

An executor's duties start with the death of the testator. One of the first duties may be to register the death and collect the death certificate. When doing this at the Registry for Births, Deaths and Marriages, a form PA2, entitled *How to obtain probate* may be given to you. Basically, the booklet tells you how to proceed with probate, who can apply for the grant and where to apply.

The simplest way of receiving all the relevant forms is to telephone your nearest Probate Registry (or Sub-Registry) and ask for the forms to be sent to you. (For a full list of Probate offices see pages 105–08.) The forms you will receive not only include the probate form but also tax declaration forms which will eventually be sent off to the Capital Taxes Office.

Depending upon the circumstances of the death, an initial medical death certificate is usually issued by the hospital authorities or the general practitioner in attendance where death occurs at home. In the case of sudden death, this is only issued once the autopsy has been carried out. The certificate, given to the closest relative or known executor, has to be sent or taken to the Registrar of Births, Deaths and Marriages within five days of the date of death. That Registrar will then issue the formal death certificate.

It is advisable to obtain extra copies of the death certificate which can be purchased at the time the original one is given, as you will need to send a copy to each company where assets are held. If you have obtained only two copies, you will have to wait for these to be returned before sending off your next letter, thus delaying the procedure.

It is unfortunate, but there are occasions when death occurs while abroad, causing added strain on the next of kin. The first thing to do is to register the death with the appropriate authority in the country where the death occurred. A death certificate should also be obtained. The British embassy or consulate in that country can help with these arrangements and in bringing the body or ashes back to the United Kingdom; you can also register the death with them.

Unless you are insured for such eventualities, the cost of bringing the body back to this country has to be borne by you and the cost can be high. The embassy or consulate can help with a small interim loan to facilitate this wish but it will only cover a tiny portion of the overall cost.

What is a grant and why is it necessary?

A grant is in effect a court order. It is your legal proof of title to deal with the estate. Without it some companies and banks will not release money or assets held in the deceased's name. The grant gives authority for these assets to be passed on to the named person to deal with.

A grant may not be necessary in certain cases; for example, if a house was jointly owned. But if the couple still had a mortgage it would be advisable to check with the building society or bank to see if the deeds were in order.

As a simple rule of thumb you may certainly need a grant if the property is solely owned by the deceased in his or her name or if the estate exceeds £5,000.

After contacting the Probate Registry you will receive a number of forms, including form PA1 from the Probate Registry. This must be completed and returned to the Registry dealing with the application by all personal applicants. The following section explains what these are.

What are all these forms for?

Once you have advised the Personal Applications Department at your local Probate Registry, the following booklets and forms will be sent out: PA2, PA1, IHT206 and IHT205.

Booklet PA2 is small but informative and assists in the completing of PA1 and in answering queries that you may have. It also lists Registry offices, so you can select the one to which you wish to apply for the grant. PA1 must be completed by all personal applicants.

The basic inheritance tax form IHT205 needs to be completed if the estate has a value of £200,000 or less. If it is worth more, you need to telephone your nearest Capital Taxes Office and request IHT210, IHT200, work sheets IHT (WS), IHT213 and supplementary notes and pages SP1 and SP2. If you are unsure whether or not the estate could be seen as an excepted estate, ask for and work through IHT12.

Guidance booklet IHT210 is well-written and, for the subject matter, easier to follow compared to previous Inland Revenue documents. If you are unsure as to the precise meaning of a particular term or have a general query, contact the information office of your local Capital Taxes Office and they will assist.

The notes to the supplementary pages SP2 are more detailed and not as well explained as IHT210. This is because they cover all the possible assets that make up an estate. If in doubt, speak to your local Capital Taxes Office.

Details of the forms sent out by the Commissary Office in Scotland or by the Capital Taxes Office are found in Chapter 11.

What happens next?

Once these forms have been completed they should be returned along with the death certificate and original will to the Personal Applications Department of the Probate Registry. It is advisable to keep a photocopy of each form for your records.

Once the staff at the Probate Registry have had a chance to look at these forms you will be invited to attend a meeting at the nearest office to confirm the accuracy of the information supplied. Usually only one visit is necessary. It is at this visit that you will be asked to swear to the correctness of the form. Any small changes can be given at this time. Once this is over and any fee and tax due have been paid a grant of probate is issued. A grant of probate will not be issued if there is any inheritance tax due or if the grant of probate fee has not been paid.

If you do not pay inheritance tax for the first six months after the end of the month in which the deceased died, then interest is charged on the amount due. This varies but the current rate is 4 per cent.

Of course, depending upon the complexities of the estate the time taken to complete these forms will vary. You may find a considerable amount of time has elapsed between asking for the forms and returning them as in the mean time you have had to assess the estate and value its assets.

A grant will not be issued if there is any objection registered in respect of the estate and will only be actioned once it has been resolved. If the objections cannot be resolved, then in all probability the matter will be referred to a judge in the Chancery Division of the courts. However, before that, the objection may be heard at the District Probate Registry to ascertain if there are any valid points.

Again, if you have any doubts about whether or not your application is suitable for a personal application, speak to the Probate Registry staff.

10

Valuing and Administering the Estate

The example of a will shown on pages 61–63 will be referred to in this chapter to take you, as an executor, through the different jobs that have to be done when valuing an estate and administering a will. The only variation to this will, of course, is that you are seen as the executor.

As an executor you will know where Edith's will is located; also general instructions, such as her wish to be buried in the local church's graveyard. Edith's estate is provisionally valued in the region of £225,000 and after stated bequests the residue or remainder has been left to her husband James. There is no mortgage on the farm and at the current (April 2000) threshold of inheritance tax there will be no inheritance tax to pay. Once this has been done and all debts settled, the half share of the farm can be conveyed to Richard, her son. Any running costs incurred during this time can be settled by the estate; see Chapter 7 for tax considerations. As a rule of thumb, however, remember that tax is payable by the individual beneficiary (unless stated to the contrary in the will) in direct proportion to the value of the gift which is in relation to the total taxable estate.

The same principle applies to a loan secured against an asset that forms part of the estate. For example, should Edith have taken out an overdraft before her death with her portfolio of shares as security against the loan, when Richard inherited the shares he would have to settle the overdraft unless Edith had stated in her will that the overdraft was to be repaid by the remainder of her estate. If Edith had left half of the portfolio to Richard and the other half to James, both would have to settle the debt in direct proportion to the value of their individual inheritance. Moreover, if Edith had intended to give the assets freely without any liability, unless she made those wishes clear in her will, her beneficiaries would have to repay any debts secured against the gifts noted in the will.

It is best to obtain a number of copies of a death certificate from the Births, Deaths and Marriages Registrar. As executor you will have a rough idea of how many certificates are required as a copy should be sent to each organisation holding Edith's assets.

Armed with these copies, you can now send letters to Edith's bank, building society, National Savings, indeed, all organisations involved. In the letter you must explain that you are the executor and that you are in the process of applying for a grant of probate. Proof of the death in the form of the death certificate should be enclosed. Request a statement of account, including interest if applicable, up to the date of death. Although not necessary if joint accounts are held, if Edith had been a single person you would have to ask the bank or building society to freeze the debits and credits going into and out of her accounts. All queries will be forwarded to you.

Another incidental job often overlooked is the redirection of post. You should arrange for a redirection of Edith's post for either three, six or 12 months. As the precise length of time of your executorial duties is not known, it is best to arrange redirection for 12 months.

How to start

Before the forms arrive you should start to make a list of all Edith's assets based on information to hand and also that information noted in her will. Do not write on the original will. Against each item you note an estimate of its value. For some of these assets this may prove difficult and so help should be sought from the appropriate source. For example, Edith had a sizeable stamp collection. Stamps are notoriously difficult to value and expert advice should be sought from a philately society or by approaching an organisation, such as Stanley Gibbons, which deals in stamps. Written valuations should always be asked for.

With these valuations to hand you can now start to prepare a more detailed inventory of Edith's estate.

Property

Although not essential, it is important to get a professional valuation on property unless you are able, on the basis of other properties nearby and recently sold, to make your own valuation. The Inland Revenue may, after the grant has been issued, decide to send round its own official, the District Valuer. He or she will value the property based on his or her own opinion of the current market price for that type of property in the area, which might differ from that considered by the estate agent to be realistic. If you do a valuation through an estate agent, you can put the lower of the two prices down. If the District Valuer thinks that it is too low, he or she can amend it upward, but should you put the higher of the two values down you are stuck with it as chances are that he or she will not reduce the amount.

Council Tax was introduced in April 1993. The tax was based on property prices which were seen as the ones prevailing two years before that date. Since then, there has been an increase in the market price of houses in most areas. Naturally, this has led to debate on property valuations and the tax subsequently charged. If in doubt, the best course of action would be to seek professional advice from surveyors, your solicitor or your local Council.

The District Valuer does not have time to come round and inspect all properties that form part of estates. But he or she will almost certainly do so if a clearly inaccurate low valuation is given.

If a house is to be sold, your own estimate will serve instead of one from an estate agent. This is because the actual value of the realised price will have to be notified to the Revenue after the sale.

In Edith's case the farm was owned with her husband as tenants-in-common, and in the directions laid out in her will her share passes on her death to her son. However, for inheritance tax purposes her share still has to be valued. It is worth noting here that should Edith have left her half share to her husband, then such a transfer between husband and wife would have been exempt for inheritance tax purposes.

Let us say that the farm was valued at £275,000; Edith's half share would be £137,500. Should there have been a mortgage, then her half share of this would have to be deducted from the value of her half of the house. So, say the mortgage was £40,000, Edith's liability under the mortgage would have been £20,000, making £117,500 of equitable value. Whoever held the mortgage to the property would have to be informed and an exact figure requested as to the outstanding mortgage at the date of death.

By value, the tax authority means the price that the property could be sold for if it were put on the open market with *vacant possession* on the day that Edith died. If the house were tenanted, then a lower value is given to take account of this restriction.

If you were not sure whether the property was held jointly, an examination of the title deeds would be necessary.

Example 1. How to calculate inheritance tax
(Note: this does not relate to Example 2.)

		£
Total value of estate, say,		260,000
Less		
Funeral expenses	1,250	
Half share of mortgage	20,000	
	21,250	238,750
Less current allowable level of inheritance tax		234,000
Total taxable estate		4,750
Inheritance tax at 40% =	£1,900	

The first valuation hurdle is over. Edith's estate is clearly solvent with her assets exceeding any liabilities. All legacies can therefore be met in full.

Now you would have to enquire whether Edith was a beneficiary of a trust or life interest from any of her ancestors or other persons' estates. If she had been, then exact details of the inheritance would have to be obtained. For this example, Edith was not a beneficiary of a trust or life interest.

The Inland Revenue normally requires the precise value of items from pensions, life and endowment policies to building society accounts. But if it is clear that the estate is a small one, then approximate valuations are accepted by the Probate Registry.

Based on the response from each organisation that you have written to, once probate has been granted, a copy of the official grant should be sent to each company for their records. All copy letters either sent to you or received by you should be kept on file.

Example 2. Inventory and valuation of Edith Baker's estate

Details	Approximate value £
Somerset Farm (value £275,000; half share £137,500)	137,500
Jewellery:	
diamond and emerald brooch	1,650
engagement ring and wedding ring	800
other jewellery	1,800
Antiques:	
grandmother clock	3,000
chaise longue	1,500
four-poster bed	2,500
2 Victorian button-back chairs	850
1 painting, early 19th century	2,500
Investments:	
National Savings certificates	8,000
Building society account (1) (account no 0000000)	3,000
Building society account (2) (account no 1111111)	2,500
Premium Bonds	500
stocks and shares (see separate list)	15,000
stamp collection	6,800
Insurance:	
endowment policy (no 000002) (with profits, to be verified)	15,500
life insurance policy (no 000332)	25,000

Other miscellaneous items		5,450
Total of estate		233,850
Value of the estate (approximate)		£233,850

Debts	£	
Funeral expenses	1,250	
Miscellaneous debts before death	1,000	
Total liabilities	2,250	
Less		
Probate fee	317	
		2,567
Approximate value for distribution		£231,283

As Edith's estate is over £200,000, IHT200 will need to be completed. This does not necessarily mean that inheritance tax is due, but rather that the figures submitted need to be checked in case it is.

Example 3. Letter requesting details on the estate's behalf

The following is a sample letter that should be sent out to each organisation holding estate assets.

---

12 Calthorpe Lane,
Bearwood,
Warwickshire BR2 2PJ

16th June 2000

The Manager
Birmingham Building Society
2B High Street
Birmingham B2 2RT

Dear Sir
I am the executor of the will of the late Edith Mary Baker of Somerset Farm, Non-Such Lane, Burton, Warwickshire who died on   day of   19xx. I am writing to request the following information as to the exact value of Mrs Baker's assets

---

held in her name with your organisation. If there are any details missing please supply them.

Account number:
Type of account:
Date account opened:
Value of account at date of death:
Interest accrued up to date of death:
Interest accrued since death up to the date of letter:
Has tax been deducted?
    If so, what amount of tax:
Since death, has tax been deducted?
    If so, what amount of tax:

I enclose a copy of Edith Baker's death certificate.

Would you please notify me of any formalities needed before you release the money to me.

Yours faithfully,

J G Person

National Savings certificates

As Edith had bought National Savings certificates you would need to obtain a claims form from your local post office. This is then filled in and sent to the address printed on the back of the leaflet. In this example, as Edith did not have much money in National Savings, you can ask for the sum held to be repaid. Each certificate number has to be noted on the form with its individual value and number of units. Also needed is the certificate's serial number and the date of issue. This action would also apply should Pensioners' Bonds be held.

Premium Bonds

When assessing Edith's Premium Bonds, if you are uncertain whether you have got all the certificates you should write in the first instance to National Savings, Government Buildings, Marton, Blackpool FY3 9YP or telephone for further information

01253 766151. This address applies if seeking information on income bonds or other government stock. But for details on National Savings Bank accounts telephone 0141 649 4555. As with all letters that you write, do quote references noted in previous correspondence. Remember to keep a copy of any letters and documents received or sent.

As Premium Bonds have a face value with no interest being paid, they do not need an official valuation, merely the number held totalled up.

Premium Bonds cannot be transferred to beneficiaries. The same is true for National Savings. Nor will the Bonds and Stock Office pay out any money to the estate without receiving the grant of probate. National Savings can transfer ownership of their various products upon receipt of proof of grant of probate, assuming the sum is over £5,000 and sending in the original certificate. If the sum is less than this and if the grant has not yet been taken out, then upon sight of the death certificate and a copy of the will the accounts can be transferred.

It is best to leave the Premium Bonds *in situ* until the final stage, just before distribution. But you must advise the Bonds and Stock Office of your address and your role as executor. Should a bond win within one year of the death, the cheque can be sent to you on behalf of the estate once probate has been granted. The money received goes directly into the executorship account for the beneficiaries.

Insurance

You should also inform the insurance companies involved of Edith's death and stop any direct debit payments currently being made to them. As Edith had a straight life policy, the company should pay out for the sum insured on proof of death, although the immediate payment depends on the value of the policy.

Edith's life insurance and endowment policies had been taken out a long time ago. The endowment policy was 'with profits', which means that in addition to the paid-up value shown on the policy there is an additional 'bonus' sum to be paid. This additional amount depends on how well the insurance company's managers have done with their investments. In your letter to the insurance company you should not only give the policy numbers but also the actual value of the policies and dates of issue. In the case of the endowment policy you should ask what the 'with profits' value is.

Edith had not invested in a pension nor had she a company pension. Again, if she had you would have to write to the company concerned, notifying them of her death and asking for a precise valuation. They in turn would require proof of death and confirmation of your role as executor.

Bank and building society accounts

As James and Edith had held a joint deposit and current account you would not need to amend any normal payments that go through as a matter of course. Joint account holders can continue to withdraw from a jointly held account. However, for inheritance tax purposes you have to obtain a balance of each account at the date of death. That amount is usually halved, in the case of accounts held jointly by husband and wife, and the proportion that belonged to the deceased will be put down on the Capital Taxes form. Accounts held by a single person would have to be noted at full value and payment into and out of these accounts would have to be stopped.

Banks and building societies would still require sight of the death certificate and perhaps the will.

You should now be receiving payments (and bills). It might be worthwhile to open an executor's account at this stage, especially if other persons are going to benefit. This will ensure that your monies are kept apart from those of the estate. In addition, the statements from the bank are a useful record of monies and expenditure. Do ask the bank what charges are likely to apply. (This charge is deducted from the residue of the estate.)

Check with both banks and building societies where Edith held an account to see whether there is a second or third account not known to you. When visiting either organisation return any bank cards or passbooks held, obtaining a receipt for each.

There are billions of unclaimed funds held by banks and building societies where people have forgotten to supply details alongside their will.

Shares and other investments

For a number of years Edith had dabbled on the stock market and had a variety of shares in her portfolio. You would have to locate the share certificates and on a separate sheet note the number and type of shares held (such as preferential or ordinary) and the names of each company found on individual certificates. (The same would apply for like investments, eg unit trusts, PEPs.) Obtain the *Financial Times* (or any of the major national daily papers) dated the day after Edith's death, and you should find buying and selling prices quoted. The value you are looking for is the lower of the two quoted, as you buy at a higher price and sell at a lower one. You value the shares by taking the lower of the two figures quoted in the *Stock Register* and adding one-quarter of the difference between the share's two prices. You can also value shares by subtracting the bid from the offer price and taking half of that figure and adding it to the lower of the quoted prices. These figures can be found in other publications; for example, the Stock Exchange publish the *Daily Official List* and main libraries hold a copy of the *Stock Register*.

If the death occurs over a weekend, you can choose to value shares either on the basis of Friday's closing price or Monday's closing value. The lower price will, of course, result in less tax and possibly lower probate fees.

Of course, if you are unhappy about valuing shares yourself, you can ask the securities department of your bank to do this. Alternatively, telephone the stockbroker who sold the shares in the first place.

Example 4. Share value list

Amount of shares held	Company	Price quoted	Value of holding
500	BW & Co Ltd	156/150	£757.50
600	KP Ordinary	172/160	£978.00
600	Plate & Co	148/140	£852.00
1000	Copper Works	222/210	£2,130.00
800	Lampshade Ltd	170/163	£1,318.00

(*Note: The names and prices above are examples only and do not relate to any known company.*)

Most shares are quoted in pence. For instance, a value quoted at, say, 578 pop pops into £5 and 78 pence. Certain high value shares, however, are quoted in pounds.

You may notice from the certificates that dividend payments are made twice yearly. To find out whether any payment is due write to the company secretary of each company concerned and ask whether any dividends are due. If you can't find dividend vouchers, ask for these at the same time. If you do not have the head office address of each company, then contact the Stock Exchange, as all quoted companies are registered there with their head office addresses noted on file.

When checking the newspaper, you might have noticed that beside the quoted price a symbol or letters are shown. 'Xd' means that the price quoted excludes the dividend value. Usually, this is noted some two weeks or so before the dividend is due. So if Edith had sold the shares with the Xd in force, she would still receive the dividend on those shares and not the person who bought them. The price quoted is, therefore, lower to take this into account.

Dividend cheques are usually sent out on the day the dividend is due but prepared beforehand.

If a rights issue had been in force it would mean that the company is issuing new shares to existing shareholders at a price lower than the current market price. In this instance a letter is sent out to all shareholders and the proportion of shares offered is based on the number of existing shares held.

A scrip issue would be noted alongside the price. Exscrip means that it is the value placed on the share while the company is issuing new shares to existing shareholders based on the percentage of their existing holding.

Edith's portfolio had not included any unit trusts. If it had, you would have to write to the unit trust companies concerned. Unlike shares, where you hold a number of shares in a particular company, for a unit trust you hold units within a trust and that trust has a specified category of investment, say, Small Company, Far East, Recovery and so on. Basically, money put into a unit trust is 'pooled' with other investors' money in the same category of trust, to purchase shares in companies fulfilling that category's definition.

TESSAs

When Tax Exempted Special Savings Accounts were introduced they did not take into account the possible death of account holders. That is now behind us. Should a TESSA account holder die, then that account ceases and the funds have to be transferred into a standard account pending grant of probate and subsequent distribution. The amount earned is deemed to be free of tax.

From April 1999 no new TESSA may be taken out. You can, however, continue with your existing TESSA.

Personal Equity Plans (PEPs)

These have proved to be a popular form of investment. You can put up to £6,000 per annum into a general PEP and £3,000 into a single-company PEP in any tax year. If the deceased owned a PEP and the estate continued to hold it in order to complete the year's investment, the above rules would apply. Thereafter the PEP would have to be closed and the money put back into the estate.

From April 1999, no future PEPs can be taken out, but provided you do not withdraw from your own, you can continue to hold it as a tax-free investment.

Individual Savings Accounts (ISAs)

These were launched on 6 April 1999. ISAs replace TESSAs and PEPs, although if you have existing investments in these prior to 6 April 1999 you will still be able to keep them on.

ISAs are supposed to be 'the' tax-free savings plan for the next ten years, ie any gain made is free from capital gains tax and any income is free from income tax. Moreover, any income received from shares will have a 10 per cent tax credit attached for the next five years. As with TESSAs and PEPS, investors must be 18 or over and be ordinarily resident in the United Kingdom.

For two years, the limit for investment is £7,000. Of this, up to £3,000 may be invested in a savings account and up to £1,000 in life insurance products. The remaining £3,000 can be invested in the stock market. Here it starts to get more complicated, in that if you do not take any of the other options, you can invest the entire £7,000 in the stock market via unit trusts, investment trusts or directly into shares.

The ISAs are split into what is now called a 'mini' or 'maxi'. With a mini ISA you can buy each part of the three allowable mini ISAs from three different providers. A maxi ISA can only be purchased from a single provider.

The Government has introduced a standard mark called CAT which stands for Cost, Availability and Terms and should now be looked at as the Government's standard of high performance. The CAT mark signifies that there are no hidden charges or penalties and that access to investor's money is easy.

Providers of ISAs have been rather slow off the mark because for one thing these investments are far more complicated than their predecessors. Select the ISA of your choice and while a CAT mark is extremely useful do ensure that past performance in other similar investments is also taken into consideration.

Other income

As she had not worked for many years, Edith had no income coming in other than the occasional dividend payment and interest from her building society accounts, deposit accounts and National Savings. You would still have to write to the Inspector of Taxes at the nearest Inland Revenue office, notifying the Revenue of her death and letting them know that the small amounts of income earned had either already been noted on James's income tax return form or noted on her own income tax return form.

Had Edith been a pensioner, her state pension allowance book would have to be returned to the nearest Department of Social Security office, whose address can be found in the telephone directory.

Hire purchase

Should a hire purchase agreement have been in force, you would have to write to the company concerned and ask for an exact assessment of the debt. In the meantime, if the agreement had been jointly signed, the surviving signatory should continue to pay the monthly instalments.

Listing the valuations

Most of the contents of the house had been jointly owned with no hire purchase scheme. Therefore it would be a matter of listing all items and placing an approximate second-hand value against each. A family car, for instance, valued at £1,000 would be apportioned to her estate at £500, in other words half the value. Should an amount of the band still be outstanding against it, then if jointly owned, the appropriate apportionment would need to be deducted.

As the jewellery had already been itemised in her will this need not be done, but the full valuation would have to be placed on the valuation sheet as Edith owned the jewellery outright. General items, such as clothes, tables, chairs, TV and so on would not need itemising but, again, a second-hand value would have to be noted. The Inland Revenue does not expect an exact and absolute value for these items down to the last pound but does expect a valuation that is sensible and realistic. Again, these general items, if jointly owned, have half of each value listed. As an example of inclusions on an inventory list, see pages 133–34.

Any cash in Edith's possession at the time of her death, whether in her handbag or in her desk drawer at home, would have to be accounted for on the valuation sheet. This loose cash could be used on the estate's behalf to purchase stamps, for example, provided it is accounted for. Any money spent personally on the funeral could be reimbursed from the estate once probate has been granted.

Let us assume that the estate, once valued, exceeds the first valuation figure. As this is only your rough guide it would not matter. What does matter, however, is that the value on the Capital Taxes form is correct.

With all the valuations to hand, the forms can be completed and despatched to the Probate Registry. In the mean time you should continue to administer the estate, collecting the debts, noting any assets that have been redeemed and keeping close account of all transactions in your own book-keeping journal.

Administering a trust

Trusts have only been briefly mentioned because of their diversity and individuality. There will usually be more than one trustee and the likelihood is that at least one will belong to a profession, such as a solicitor or accountant. Trusts should state whether or not trustees in a profession or business will be able to charge for their time and any incurred expenses.

Some trusts are simple and therefore quite easy to deal with, while the reverse is also true. However, the principles of investing a trust's assets are similar whether a trust has £100,000 or £500,000 to invest. What does matter is keeping the trust's expenses to a minimum, keeping accurate records of the financial affairs of the trust and investing in financial markets that are able to produce a reasonable income, but as important is to safeguard capital and its growth from unsafe investments and underlying inflation.

The following paragraphs are only meant as a general guide. In most instances a trust is written so that it is within the Trustees Act, which is there to protect the trust's assets and ultimately the beneficiaries. It allows for a certain proportion of money to be held in a narrow range band of investments with the remainder in a broad range band. It does not allow for speculative, risky investments such as commodity futures. Should a trust be written outside the confines of this Act, then as a beneficiary or one of the trustees it would be recommended that you seek independent legal advice. The trustees are by law obliged to follow exactly the wishes of a trust.

As a trustee, before considering investing monies for the trust, examine the following carefully. What does the trust state? What are the life tenant's and residuary beneficiaries' wishes? What are their ages and needs? What has the will specified? For example, should the life tenant be an elderly person, ie over 85 years of age, then long-term investment bonds bought over par (ie at a capital loss) would perhaps be unsuitable. Would the residuary beneficiaries be interested to continue any long-term government bonds after the death of the life tenant? Has capital appreciation or specific income been stated in the will? And do the proposed investments allow for this? Remember, expenses and underlying inflation can erode a trust's investments.

If there is any doubt as to a trustee's impartiality or should there have been any possible illegal acts, then the residuary beneficiary and the other beneficiaries may be able to sue the trustees for any loss. This is expensive and time-consuming.

Under the new self-assessment rules, each trustee can make a return and in turn each will be liable for any errors or omissions made that result in any loss of tax due to the Revenue.

Shire Horse Society

Patron: Her Majesty The Queen

The Society has been responsible for over 100 years for the promotion of the Shire horse and the maintenance of the Stud Book. In more recent years the conservation and development of the breed – part of our national heritage – has become a greater priority.

The society actively encourages the breeding and use of Shire horses throughout the country. There are Shire horse classes at over 180 affiliated Shows.

As a result of the Society's endeavours, the Shire horse is currently enjoying an upsurge in the interest among overseas buyers, particularly in Europe and the United States.

Further information can be obtained from:

Tonie Gibson, OBE, Chief Executive
Shire Horse Society, East of England Showground,
Peterborough, PE2 6XE
Tel: 01733 234 451 Fax: 01733 370 038
Registered Charity No: 210619
Company Limited by Guarantee No: 12383
Email: info@eastofengland.org.uk
http://www.shire-horse.org.uk

11

What Happens in Scotland?

In most cases you will have had prior notice of your task as executor. However, it is worth noting at the outset that in Scotland, except where an estate does not exceed £25,000 gross (as of 1 April 1999) and is known as a small estate (see below), in the majority of cases a solicitor's service or that of a licensed executing practitioner is used. This chapter, therefore, briefly notes procedures in Scotland, explaining the different terminology used, and highlights areas of major differences.

The first thing to do after the death, wherever you live in the United Kingdom, is to find the will. It may have been lodged with the deceased's bank, solicitor or hidden away at the family home. Although a photocopy of a will cannot be substituted for the original – except for an action of a declarator to prove the terms of the will, where the original document has been lost, brought in the Court of Session – it is advisable to have a photocopy for your own reference.

What is a 'small estate'?

In Scotland a special procedure is followed if an estate is under £25,000 gross. The legal term for this size of estate is a *small estate*. For estates that exceed this value this involves, in intestate cases, a petition to the court for appointment of an *'executor dative'*. Presentation (inventory of estate and petition) is rarely made by personal application; instead, it is presented by a solicitor or a licensed executing practitioner.

The staff at the Commissary Offices throughout Scotland will process small estates provided that complications do not arise. If they are able to assist, they require full and detailed information regarding the estate and its assets. In calculating the value of the estate, debts such as funeral expenses, gas or electricity bills, hire purchase payments and any outstanding mortgage must be disregarded. The applicant must supply information to the staff at the Commissary Office, making a list and supporting this list by documentation. All property must be included in this list, even accounts held jointly.

In addition to a list of assets, you would also have to supply a death certificate, a divorce certificate, if applicable, and a will. If there is no will, the court will appoint the closest relative in order of 'preferred' status, namely spouse, child, brother or sister, parent.

As in England, there is no charge made by the Sheriff Clerk in giving advice or information or for completing the inventory or forms on an applicant's behalf. Again as in England, there is a statutory fee charged whether a solicitor is used or not and this is calculated on the basis of the gross value of the estate. For an estate of £5,000 or under no fee is charged and between £5,001 and £50,000 the fee is £72; for estates where the gross value is £50,001 and above the fee is £103.

In all intestate cases other than a surviving spouse case you will be asked to obtain a *bond of caution* (type of insurance policy against any mistakes or misappropriation of the funds) from an insurance company, before you are able to take on the task.

Information needed
Bank and building society accounts
The passbooks must be presented to the companies for updating. Any interest accrued up to the date of death must be noted by the manager in pencil. If you cannot find a passbook, write to the bank or building society concerned and ask them to supply you with a letter stating the type of account, the account number and the value plus interest, noted separately.

Insurance policies
The insurance company must be asked to supply details of the policy, its value, its number and any bonuses applicable.

*National Savings Bank (including National Savings certificates
and Grannie bonds)*

A letter must be obtained from the Director of Savings giving
the value of each holding, including interest, up to the date of
death. This address will be found on the reverse of the claim
form which you obtain from your local post office. (National
Savings, Marton, Blackpool, Lancs FY3 9YP. Tel 01253
766151.)

Premium Bonds

If the actual bonds cannot be produced, then the holder's registration number should be given. If this also cannot be found,
write to the address on page 120 and ask for confirmation of
the numbers, stating why you need them.

Stocks and shares

The valuation route as found on page 123 needs to be followed
and should include the value of the item, plus dividends. If a
stockbroker or bank is used, ask them to confirm these details in
writing.

Heritable property

This includes a house, shop, land, etc. A valuation from an
estate agent, solicitor or other appropriate person must be
obtained, again in writing. It is advisable, where heritable property forms part of an estate, for a solicitor's services to be used.

Rights

There are two rights given: first, prior rights and, second, legal
rights. Prior rights means just that – the spouse has a right to
the property and these rights must be satisfied before legal
rights; legal rights allow for what is legally available to a spouse
or descendant; see page 137 for further clarification.

Once you are sure that all the information and its supportive
evidence is to hand, you need to arrange an interview with the
Commissary Office. At the end of the interview all offices
require that you make a declaration that the information given
by you is 'full and true'. If the deceased died intestate, in some

offices you would need to bring two witnesses to the interview to swear on your behalf that you are who you say you are and that your relationship to the deceased is as you say. One witness must not be related to either the deceased or the applicant and the other witness, although a relative is allowable, must not be a beneficiary.

Tax forms
There are four tax forms in Scotland which double as an inventory of estate on which confirmation is granted.

Form Cap B-3 (1989) is an Inland Revenue Scotland form for small estates. On page 2 of the form the applicant has to make a declaration that the information given is full and true. The same applies on Form B4 (1989) for excepted estates.

Lastly, there is Form Cap A3 for estates other than 'small estates' or 'excepted estates' which is sent with its own instruction booklet and Form Cap D-1 (1977) for corrective or additional inventory belonging to the estate.

Estate checklist

An estate checklist, reproduced by courtesy of the Commissary Office in Edinburgh, is shown below. Indeed, this list could be used as a guide for those preparing an inventory of an estate in England, Wales or Northern Ireland. It is stressed, however, that this list is not exhaustive, merely an indication of how detailed the inventory should be. Details of each item, along with its current value at date of death, should accompany the list. As follows:

Bank and building society accounts including Post Office Giro
Insurance policies
Premium Bonds
Savings bonds (including index-linked 'Grannie bonds')
National Savings certificates
Old age pension
Invalidity pension
DSS death grant
Pension from employer

Holiday pay outstanding
Salary outstanding
Employer's death grant (gratuity)
Employer's superannuation
Mobility allowance
Shares, including those in co-operatives
Stocks and shares (eg Treasury Stock, consolidated and public
    stock, etc)
Repayment of TV licence stamps
Overpayment of rent, Council Tax (including rebates)
Gift vouchers
Estate abroad
Trust estate
Income from a trust
Rents from property
Beneficiary under someone else's will
Personal effects
Motor car
Cash in hand (including in hospital, nursing home, etc)
Income tax repayment
Royalties
Repayment of club subscriptions (and motoring organisations)
Repayment of loans to clubs
House, garage
Business
Strip of land
Feu duty (superiority): Ground burdens
Livestock

What does it all mean?

It is important to understand what is meant by certain legal words and phrases as some of these differ between Scotland and England. For example, in Scotland, what is meant by 'the house' or 'the furnishings' in the context of the surviving spouse's prior rights? The house is the home of the deceased in which the surviving spouse was in residence at the date of death. Furnishings mean any item of furniture owned by the deceased not including cars, jewellery or money.

Should a will have been written appointing you as an executor, you would be referred to as an '*executor nominate*'. As in England, if you find that you cannot fulfil your appointment for one reason or another you would have to sign a statement officially declining your role. You might be the only executor and, if so, you must ask another person to act as executor and you must wait until he or she assumes this role before resigning from your office.

In Scotland, if a person dies without a will, the court appoints an executor known as an '*executor dative*'. Just as in England, the duty of an executor dative is to collect, administer and distribute the assets according to the intestacy laws.

There are two types of estate: heritable (meaning house, buildings, land) and moveable (meaning furniture, cash, etc). An estate usually has both, as the majority of people now own their own home.

The final value of a house is determined once any outstanding debts, ie mortgage or home improvement loan, have been paid. If the deceased has died intestate, then the value of the house up to £110,000 goes to the surviving spouse. Before 26 November 1993 the figure of £65,000 applied and it still does for deaths before that date.

If a house has a survivorship destination clause in the title deeds, whoever is the survivor of this clause inherits the property; see below under 'Heritable property'.

Children

Prior to 26 November 1968, a child born out of a marriage and not mentioned specifically in a will could not normally inherit from his or her parents if the beneficiaries of the will were referred to as 'my children'. The illegitimate child could only claim legal rights if the will was executed on or after 26 November 1968, and refers to 'children'. Illegitimate children are included unless, for instance, there is reference such as to 'lawful children'.

The legal application of the word 'child' or 'children' in Scotland refers to children of a marriage, adopted children and now illegitimate children *but not* stepchildren. For stepchildren to be included in distribution of an estate the will has specifically to state the legacy along with the child's name.

A child under 16 cannot legally accept a legacy him or herself. Rather the legacy has to be given to the parents or guardians on the child's behalf for the purpose of investing, but only in secure investments. If the legacy is of £20,000 or more, the approval of the Auditor of Court must be obtained first. The parents or guardians would have to sign the receipt for the legacy.

Once the child has reached the age of 16 years, he or she would be able to receive the entire legacy, including any interest earned.

Heritable property

If a property is owned by two people with the title deed drawn to include a survivorship destination clause, despite what is written in the will the house will automatically pass to the surviving owner without the property included in the confirmation to the deceased's estate. However, this does not apply if the destination has been recalled by the deceased in his or her lifetime, or if the deceased had provided the whole purchase price. In such cases, the property must be confirmed and the title transferred by the executors to the heir.

Where property is bequeathed to a person under a will, or where it is passing to a person under the intestate succession rules, the title to the property can be transferred to the executors by signing a document appropriately called a 'docket'. A solicitor or licensed executing practitioner would have to draw one up for you.

A docket contains the name(s) of the executor(s), the name of the deceased, and the name of the person to whom the property is being transferred. It has also to state what rights are involved, ie whether he or she has prior rights or legal rights to the property and whether it is part of the gift as noted in the will. The full address of the house must also be included. If the house is going to be sold, a document granting legal title to the purchaser called a 'disposition' will have to be prepared, again by a solicitor or licensed conveyancing practitioner.

Intestate estate

Before 1964 the intestacy rules regarding the distribution to the surviving spouse and children were somewhat unfair. However, in 1964, the Succession (Scotland) Act effectively altered the existing intestacy rules.

Where there is a surviving spouse, by right he or she is entitled to be the sole executor of the estate. If the estate exceeds the prior rights, then other entitled persons may act.

There are two further terms, already mentioned, peculiar to Scottish law: 'prior rights' and 'legal rights'. 'Prior rights' means that the surviving spouse has a 'right' to the deceased's house. From 26 November 1993 the value of items under prior rights are as follows: house £110,000; furniture £20,000 (excluding the car); and a cash right (paid out of the heritable estate and the moveable estate) worth £30,000 if there was issue, and £50,000 if there was no issue.

If there is an outstanding balance on the mortgage, the surviving spouse receives the value of the house less any outstanding mortgage. This is so even if an endowment policy formed part of the estate to pay off the mortgage upon death.

Where the furnishings of the house exceed £20,000, the surviving spouse is entitled to choose furnishings up to the value of £20,000. Again, the value received is limited to the value in the estate.

It is worth noting that a car, jewellery or money are not included in the term 'furnishings' and furnishings do not necessarily have to be located in the deceased person's home.

After prior rights have been satisfied then 'legal rights' apply. Legal rights are taken from that part of the estate that remains after debts and prior rights have been paid.

In Scotland, even with a will, you cannot absolutely exclude your spouse or children from inheriting part of your moveable estate, as they have a 'legal right' to part of it. If a spouse and children survive, the spouse takes one-third and the children one-third. If there is a surviving spouse but no children, then the spouse takes half. If there is no surviving spouse, the children take half. Only the remaining one-third or one-half of the estate may be disposed of by the testator. However, the heritable estate may be disposed of as the testator wishes.

The estate that remains after both prior rights and legal rights have been satisfied is known as 'free estate'. This portion is distributed according to the laws of intestate succession to the children or to other relatives of the deceased.

The order of succession to the free estate is (1) children; (2) parents/brother and sister (equal share of the estate); (3) brothers or sisters if there are no parents or (4) parents if there are no brothers or sisters; (5) surviving spouse; (6) uncles, aunts; (7) other living traceable family members generation by generation. If a member of a particular category predeceased the deceased leaving issue, such issue share their parents' entitlement. If no relative can be traced, despite extensive searches by the executor dative, the estate goes to the Crown once all expenses and debts have been paid.

Does divorce alter a will?

In England if a person makes out a will and then subsequently marries and divorces, the granting of the 'decree absolute' will make the will invalid. In Scotland, however, this does not apply; neither marriage nor divorce invalidates a will.

An interesting point arises from this. If you do not make out a new will setting aside gifts or money to your new spouse, she will not benefit under your old will. There is a way around this, however. The new spouse can claim legal rights which would entitle her to one-third (or if you have no children, one-half) but of the moveable estate only. She could not claim the house.

Debts

There are three categories of debt in Scotland: 'secured debts' (ie overdraft, mortgage), 'privileged debts' (funeral expenses, council tax), and 'ordinary debts' (butcher, baker and candlestick maker). You can pay secure debts and privileged debts as and when the money is available, but ordinary debts have to wait until the estate is finalised, usually six months after the date of death.

For the purpose of division of the estate, debts can only be applied to its equivalent source of estate. In other words a loan against the house (heritable) can only be set against that source. Similarly, expenses such as telephone bills and funeral expenses must be paid out of the moveable estate.

This is where matters start to get complicated: calculating the net moveable estate or heritable property and working out the legal rights and so on. It is, therefore, not within the scope of this book to elucidate further and you would be well advised to involve a solicitor or licensed executing practitioner in practice in Scotland.

Useful addresses

Payment of stamp duty
Controller of Stamps (Scotland)
Mulberry House
16 Picardy Place
Edinburgh EH1 3AB

Registrar of Deeds
Registers of Scotland
Meadowbank House
153 London Road
Edinburgh EH8 7AU
(0131 659 6111)

HM Commissary Office
27 Chambers Street
Edinburgh EH1 1LB
(0131 225 2525)

Supplier of inheritance tax inventory forms
Capital Taxes Office
Mulberry House
16 Picardy Place
Edinburgh EH1 3AB
(0131 524 3000)

Forms can also be obtained from main post offices throughout Scotland.

12

Winding Up an Estate

The first thing that usually crosses an executor's mind is the release of the house. As more and more people have now purchased their own home this usually means that there is a mortgage to consider. For mortgages that are linked to insurance policies the amount outstanding on death is automatically paid off.

Property

The first thing that has to be looked at is the title of the house. If it is in joint ownership, then it usually (but not always) passes to the survivor. You should consult your solicitor, building society or bank if they hold the deeds in order to establish the exact position, and a charge to the estate for this service will be made. However, if the house is going to a named beneficiary, then, in certain instances, the building society or bank may agree to that person taking over the existing mortgage or remortgaging the house.

If there are not sufficient assets for distribution, you might have to put the house up for sale. Once it has been sold and the mortgage paid off, then the remaining amount can be distributed.

Upon request, the building society or bank will let you know the amount outstanding on the mortgage. When a house has a mortgage this fact is noted on a charge certificate which shows all relevant title details, including who the current registered owner is. The paper certifies that the building society or bank has the house as security for the money it has loaned. Once the mortgage has been paid off the certificate is released.

On receipt of this certificate – sent on a special Land Registry form – send it on to the Land Registry, which will cross out the details of the mortgage and return the land certificate, as it is now called, to the executor. This is formal proof that ownership of the house is free from any loan commitments.

In rare instances a half share of a property may be transferred to the other joint owner with an agreement drawn up to state that the person can continue to live in that abode, known as an interest in possession. So despite giving it away, if interest in possession exists this half share still has to be accounted for on the inheritance tax forms less, of course, any liabilities. For inheritance tax, interest in possession is seen as an ineffective transfer and the seven-year rule would not apply, ie the total of the property has to be included.

The Land Registry notes all property transactions throughout the United Kingdom. The Registry has details of approximately 15.5 million registered properties in England and Wales and estimates that there are a further 6.5 million properties still to be registered. Obviously, if the property that you are concerned with is not registered, then the Land Registry holds no information. To find out if the property is registered, the Registry has a series of maps called the Public Index Map, which not only tells you if the property is registered but shows the extent of land in every registered title. This Map is open to inspection at no cost unless it is more than ten titles. It is worthwhile noting that since 3 December 1990 anyone can obtain information on a property that is registered, even if they are not the owners.

As executor, once probate has been given, you have to notify the Land Registry (offices in most towns and large cities, see your local telephone directory for the one nearest you) that the title of the property is now transferred to the ownership of the executors, in other words the estate. The house can be transferred directly to one of the beneficiaries but a further application – on the same form – has to be sent off to the Registry. Instead of the mortgage showing the names of the executors, the name of the ultimate beneficiary has to be inserted.

The Land Registry form can be obtained by asking for Form AF1 Assent or Approbation from either the Land Registry office nearest to you or from most bookshops. A leaflet entitled

Explanatory Leaflet No. 15 is available which contains general
Land Registry information. If you are using the services of a
solicitor this process will be undertaken on your behalf.

You should note on the form the title number, the address of
the property concerned, the date, the names of the executors
(and their addresses) as well as the name and address of the
deceased. The form must be witnessed, with the witness sup-
plying his or her full address and occupation.

Land Registry fees

The Land Registry charges a fee based on the value of the
house whether the house has been transferred to the beneficiary
or bought outright. This fee is known as Scale 2.

Table 12.1 – Land Registry Scale 2 charges

£0–£100,000	£40
£100,001–£200,000	£50
£200,001–£500,000	£70
£500,001–£1,000,000	£100
£1,000,001 and above	£200

What to do if you cannot find a title deed

If you are unable to locate a title deed or a mortgage certificate
and you doubt whether the house is registered, you should go to
the Land Registry, where you should be able to inspect details
pertaining to the property. Upon proof of your role as executor,
the Land Registry would be able to send a replacement of the lost
title deed. As a rule of thumb, however, if there is no loan certificate or charge certificate, then the title is not registered. This is
still possible as compulsory registration has only been introduced
relatively recently. Indeed, in certain areas it means that some
houses that have not been sold have not been registered.

Among the deceased's papers there may be a copy of the
original conveyance sent by the solicitor at the time the house
was purchased. This conveyance was the official document
transferring ownership from the previous owner to the
deceased. In the case of leasehold property the conveyance is
called an assignment.

Transferring ownership

Once you have this deed, you are able to prepare a document transferring ownership, whether as instructed in the will or as administrator in the case of intestacy. Again, as with the normal transfer of a registered property, the building society or bank will give back the title deed to the property once the mortgage has been repaid. Attached to the mortgage deed will be an acknowledgement stating that the money has been paid off and the mortgage discharged. This deed will also include a copy of the deed of conveyance when the house was originally purchased by the deceased.

In order to make up an assent, the title deeds must accompany the deed of conveyance along with the original grant of probate or administration. On the assent form you need to show the full details pertaining to the property, ie full address, the name and full address of the person to whom the property is being transferred, legal proof that the person died, the date of death and the date that probate was granted. When returned to you, the forms are said to be 'assented'. This assent form should always be kept with the title deeds to the property.

A house held in joint ownership, ie as joint tenants passing by survivorship, is more straightforward and no assent should be needed. A death certificate is proof that the survivor is now entitled to the property along with the deeds and should be sufficient. However, if you are the beneficiary yourself, you are, in effect, writing an assent to yourself. If you are representing a number of people, then an assent form should be used.

Leasehold property

The 'landlord' or leaseholder of leasehold property has to be notified that an assent is being done and may charge a fee, but this depends on the terms of the lease. He or she may also be entitled to retain a copy of the assent. On the form all details of the lease have to be noted, such as its length, what costs are attributed to it, etc.

Leasehold property starts its life usually with 99 years noted on the title deeds. As time marches on so the lease's expiry date comes closer to completion. When this occurs the property reverts back to the owner (or landlord) of the lease, but until that time you own the leasehold property and can sell it on. However, the owner of the freehold on the property has to be informed of any lease transfer taking place. The same form for the transfer of ownership of freehold property is used.

When the beneficiary eventually comes to sell the house the original grant of probate, along with the assent, may need to be shown to prove legal ownership.

Because these property transfers can be fraught with danger when the beneficiary comes to sell – especially if the property is unregistered – it would be best to approach a solicitor and ask him or her to deal with matters. Instances have occurred when, at the final stage of selling a house, the purchaser's solicitor has noted that the property had not been legally transferred and the sale has been halted.

Bookkeeping

As an executor, it is your duty to keep a careful record of all amounts of money, property and any outstanding debts. This naturally necessitates bookkeeping.

You should keep a ledger noting all the amounts of money paid out, such as funeral expenses, telephone calls, train fares, petrol, stationery, even down to the last postage stamp. Keep a receipt for each item of expenditure and cross-reference this receipt with the same number noted in the ledger. Assets that have been sold in preparation for distribution should be noted on a separate page, stating when and to whom they were sold, the amount received for each item and where the money is now.

Money could be held on deposit and, if so, any interest payments received must also be included.

Dividend payments should also be noted along with any shares or other investments that have subsequently been sold. All of these will have vouchers which must be kept safely and again cross-referenced to the ledger.

Any tax that has been deducted from dividends or interest payments must be noted on your ledger, as eventually a repayment situation could arise. Interestingly, although an investment tax on gains made on share transactions (known as stamp duty) is payable, provided the beneficiary of the shares is also an

executor of the will, a letter of bequest can be granted with the result that there is no stamp duty to pay.

It cannot be stressed too often that accurate and detailed books need to be kept. As an executor you can be asked up to 12 years after the date your duty first commenced to show what payments were received and what distributions were made. If you keep accurate accounts it is unlikely that any charge of maladministration can be levied against you.

It is a good idea to keep back a certain amount of money in case further payments need to be made, but, more importantly, it keeps the estate liquid. There is a further example of the benefit in doing this. Suppose there is an existing business and the expenses of that business are higher than the interest being received. If there is no liquidity, certain assets may have to be sold and the best possible price may not be obtained. Another example is that a beneficiary might need payment before final distribution takes place or perhaps creditors may need an interim or complete payment.

By keeping accurate accounts you can quickly pull together all the transactions once completion has taken place and the final winding-up procedure account-wise will be relatively simple.

Tax returns

As executor of the estate you are responsible for completing income tax returns on the estate's behalf. As there is no individual concerned, then no personal tax relief is granted. For income tax purposes, the only relief that an estate can claim back is if it has had to obtain a loan from a bank in order to pay inheritance tax or the probate fee.

Before distribution, you have to fill in an income tax return form showing your calculation of how much tax is due based on the income received. This form should be signed and returned to the Revenue, who, if they agree with it, will send you a demand for the estate tax due. Once this tax has been paid, distribution can take place. Always ask the Revenue for a receipt of any tax paid as proof of the discharge of the estate's income tax liability.

When completing the income tax return you need to insert the period of administration. It is hoped that the winding-up

British Trust for Ornithology

Room 110C, The Nunnery, Thetford, Norfolk. IP24 2PU

Tel: 01842 750050 Fax: 01842 750030

Registered Charity No. 216652   Registered in England and Wales No. 357284

There are over 7,000 keen Garden BirdWatch members who record the common birds in their gardens throughout the year. They provide vital information on the ups and downs of our common birds. For more information on how to take part in Garden BirdWatch, contact Jacky Prior at the address above.

The British Trust for Ornithology is the leading research organisation studying the UK's birds and their habitats. Since 1933, tens of thousands of BTO volunteers have monitored the bird populations throughout the UK. The unique partnership of fieldworkers, survey organisers and scientists, based at our Thetford headquarters, enables the BTO to shape the future of bird conservation throughout the country and beyond.

procedure will not take longer than a year, but for each new tax year it enters, a new income tax return form must be filled in.

Any shares or unit trusts that have been sold must be included on this form and shown in the following order:

1. Number of shares sold.
2. Value of shares (in other words, how much did you receive from the sale?).
3. The date of the sale.
4. Any commissions or costs that were incurred.

This procedure has to be followed for each set of company shares sold. At the bottom of each entry you have to insert what money was made. You should insert what price the shares were bought at, less the price they were sold at, less commission charges and stamp duty.

If the shares have risen in value, then you have to show the gain. Alongside the details write the phrase 'exempt £7,100',* which refers to the amount of annual allowable capital gain before tax. (For tax year 2000/01 this exemption rises to £7,200 and for Trustees it increases to £3,600.) Any loss that has been made can be set off against any other capital gain that the estate might have made.

Once the tax forms have been filled in they should be returned to the Inland Revenue, along with a letter formally giving notice that the administration of the estate has been closed, and giving the exact date when the completion of the estate occurred. Any tax credits due from dividends must be included and reimbursement asked for. As there may be residuary beneficiaries of the will you can ask for a tax form, R185E, to be sent to you on their behalf. One form per person is needed. Remember to ask for confirmation that the Revenue have closed the estate's file and ask that any dividend folios sent to them are returned, as you will need these as evidence when preparing the final distribution.

The forms should then be returned to you together with any repayment. But it is one thing to owe the Revenue money and quite another to collect it. The Revenue ask you to pay within 30 days.

* This exempt figure is the allowance given per person for 1999/2000.

Wood Green Animal Shelters

Wood Green Animal Shelters has cared for homeless, abandoned and mistreated animals for over 75 years, since its foundation in 1924. The shelters, in Cambridgeshire, Hertfordshire and North London, aim to provide the best possible care for the thousands of animals taken in each year, and to find them new homes wherever possible.

Many pet owners worry about what will happen when they die, or are unable to continue to care for their animals. The Wood Green *Pet Alert Scheme* has been developed in response to this concern. Registration costs nothing and offers peace of mind to caring owners, especially if they are elderly or living alone.

The charity could not continue its work without the kindness of people supporting us through donations and legacies. By remembering us in their Will, people can help secure a better future for their pets and thousands of other animals in need.

Wood Green Animal Shelters
King's Bush Farm, London Road
Godmanchester,
Cambridgeshire PE18 8LJ

Tel:01480 830014; Fax: 01480 830158

Website: www.woodgreen.org.uk
Registered Charity No. 298348

149

Accounts

After gaining probate, all assets and liabilities can be settled and on doing this the estate is considered to be complete. The legacies can now be distributed.

Should you have incurred expenses as executor you will now be able to reimburse yourself out of the executorship bank account. If the will states that executors should be paid for their time, then that account can also be settled.

All beneficiaries should now receive a letter from you stating that the estate is ready for distribution and that their legacy can be collected.

Distributing legacies

As an executor you are responsible for ensuring that there are no loose ends. Therefore, each legacy that is handed over to the beneficiary must be signed for. The receipt should contain the following:

(a) details of the sum of money or description of the legacy;
(b) full details of the estate's executors;
(c) who the gift was given to under the terms of the deceased's will;
(d) the signature of the person who received the legacy.

A copy of this receipt should be kept for your records and the other copy retained by the beneficiary.

A slight problem arises if a beneficiary is under the age of 18. Legally a child cannot sign a receipt. In order to overcome this problem, the father or mother or lawful guardian should sign on the child's behalf with the proviso that when the beneficiary reaches the age of majority he or she will receive the money or gift plus any interest earned.

It is worth noting that a child under the age of 18 can also receive an income tax allowance as a single person. So it is not tax efficient for any sums of money to be placed in savings accounts where tax is deducted at source unless the interest earned in a year is likely to exceed £4,385 (2000/01). Banks and building societies now automatically deduct basic rate tax

from monies held with them unless a form is signed that states that you are not liable to tax and therefore no tax should be deducted. Any tax deducted can be reclaimed from the individual's tax office once proof has been established that he or she is not liable to pay income tax. The Revenue would require a Total Income Schedule, noting all income received together with supporting certificates, vouchers or pay slips. Alternatively, you should open an account where money is paid gross and not net; for example, with National Savings accounts.

Once all the pecuniary legacies have been paid, the executor can re-examine whether any creditors have been overlooked or, for that matter, anything of relevance to the estate. The time should be used for double-checking that everything that should have been done has been done. Once you are happy that this is the case then final accounts can be prepared.

Final accounts

If the bookkeeping has been done accurately it will be a straightforward matter to pull all the accounts together. Each sheet of accounts should be clearly headed, noting the period of administration, the deceased person's name and the type of account to be found on the sheet.

Capital accounts

The first and prime account sheet is the capital account. On one side this shows what the asset values were on the date of death, eg property less outstanding mortgage, the value of any life insurance policies, pension premiums, building society or bank accounts, National Savings, shares, retirement pensions and so on. It itemises all assets and their value and then any debts, noted on the other side of the sheet, are deducted from this amount. Debts include probate fees, inheritance tax, bank charges, Land Registry fee and so on.

Looking at the last bank statement, you should see if the amount agrees with the total amount shown in your calculations. If so, this is the final and true account. If not, then you must go over the accounts again until they are reconciled.

Income account

The income account is the next sheet that needs to be completed. It should include any income received throughout the period of administration. In other words, any dividends that have been paid, any profits paid on the trust, any interest paid on the bank account, etc, less the amount of tax deducted at source. Not only are receipts shown in the income account but also any payments that have been made; for example, mortgage repayment. The final figure shown should match exactly the final figure given on the income tax return form.

Also to be included on the income account sheet is any tax repayment made to the estate.

Distributions sheet

The last sheet to be completed is the distributions sheet. Again, all details pertaining to the estate need to be noted.

At the top of the sheet insert the remaining amount of money still held by the estate. This figure will be found in the capital account sheet. All payments made out to the beneficiaries need to be itemised, even if they include a house and contents, shares or unit trusts or the residue in the bank account. Each beneficiary in receipt of a legacy must have his or her name and what he or she is receiving noted here and its value. The total figure should match exactly with the receipts brought across from the capital and income sheets.

The closing stages

It is recommended that the distribution of the estate, unless it is a small and uncomplicated one, should not be completed under a six-month period. This is because a claimant can come forward up to six months from the date probate was granted. There are special circumstances where the time limit may be extended by the court.

If the estate has already been distributed, the executors could be looking at a court case whereby the claimant can state that he or she was not treated equally or that his or her claim was not considered when it should have been.

Once all the accounts have been written up, the beneficiaries are entitled to have the opportunity to study them, if they so wish. They might have certain questions regarding the distribution, tax or interest payment, all need to be answered. When each beneficiary has seen the accounts and agreed them, each person must sign the bottom of all account sheets.

Once cheques have been given to the beneficiaries and your receipts filed safely away, write to the bank advising that all payments have been made and that the executorship account should now be closed. Usually banks charge fees for handling administrative work. This fee will be deducted from the money held in the account. Whatever money is left is given to the residuary beneficiary unless there is a life interest (trust).

All papers together with the signed copy of the account should be placed in a safe place along with the probate certificates.

Example 1. Capital accounts

Estate accounts covering the period of administration from date of death 10 October 1997 to 5 April 1998.

Receipts	£
Somerset Farm	137,500
Contents	2,500
Antiques	10,350
Jewellery	4,250
Stamp collection	6,800
National Savings certificates	8,000
Building society account (1)	3,000
Building society account (2)	2,500
Half share of bank account	150
Premium Bonds	500
Life insurance policy	25,000
Endowment policy (with profits)	15,500
Stocks and shares (see separate list)	15,000
Cash	400
Interest paid on building society accounts	150
Gain on shares sold	2,050
Interest on National Savings	200
	233,850

Less Payments

Funeral account	1,250
Probate fee	334
Bank charges	35
Executor's expenses	145
Debts outstanding at death	1,000
Solicitor's fees	1,600
Legacies paid	1,000
Debts paid from the estate	5,364
Balance of estate to distribution account	228,486

(Note £1,000 of legacy has already been paid)

Signatures:

Executor . . . .   Approved by . . . .

Date   . . . .

Note: The figures shown are approximations.

* The Inheritance Tax Threshold applies at the rate at date of death, ie 40 per cent – £234,000 (2000/01).

Appendix 1

Probate Checklist

1. Register death and obtain death certificate (additional copies if necessary) from the nearest Registrar of Births, Deaths and Marriages.
2. If the deceased left instructions for organ donation, make sure that this request is passed on to the medical staff.
3. If directed under the will, consider funeral arrangements.
4. Collect the will. Obtain photocopies. If the deceased died intestate, consider whether you want to apply to administer the estate. If so, obtain the necessary forms from the Personal Applications Department of the nearest Probate Registry.
5. Do you need a grant of probate for an existing will or letters of administration in the case of intestacy? Ask the Probate Registry to send you the forms.
6. Collect details of all assets and liabilities for valuation purposes. Write off to relevant institutions including banks confirming the death, your position and asking for a valuation up to the date of death and whether tax has been deducted. If the estate is insolvent see a solicitor immediately.
7. Prepare a valuation sheet for the approximate value of all items in the estate. Start bookkeeping ledgers.
8. Ascertain from your valuation sheet whether or not the estate is valued at £180,000 or less, as for inheritance tax purposes it may qualify as an 'excepted estate'.
9. If the deceased was a beneficiary under a trust or life interest, ask the relevant person what each trust or life interest is, including its value and terms and if necessary seek legal advice.

10. Start to collect all assets. Fill in forms.
11. Return all forms to the Probate Registry along with the death certificate and any relevant valuations.
12. Confirm date of appointment given to you by the Probate Registry.
13. Arrange finance if necessary to pay for inheritance tax, probate fee.
14. Attend Probate Registry, swear forms, pay probate fee, if necessary pay inheritance tax.
15. Receive grant of probate or letters of administration.
16. If necessary, put a statutory advertisement in local or national papers asking for creditors and other claimants against the estate to reply. Seek legal advice if necessary.
17. If property has been valued by the valuation officer from the Inland Revenue, agree the declared value. Additional inheritance tax might have to be paid.
18. Complete income tax forms and capital gains tax forms for the period of administration.
19. Apply for and get inheritance tax discharge certificate.
20. Either through loan or through available cash in the estate, pay off any estate liabilities.
21. Pay and transfer any legacies, obtaining receipts.
22. Prepare the final estate accounts with the appropriate tax deduction certificate, R185E.
23. If the will provides for life interests or trusts, seek legal advice, as the part of the estate allocated to this will now need transferring over to the trustees.
24. Obtain approval of accounts and receipts from beneficiaries.
25. Distribute assets to beneficiaries or residuary beneficiary and obtain receipts.
26. Write to the bank, closing the bank account.

Appendix 2

Probate Fees Payable by a Personal Applicant in England and Wales

The amount of the fee payable depends on the size of the estate involved and cannot be worked out until the details are confirmed at the interview. The table below is a guide only for estates before 26 April 1999.

Net estate £	Fee £	
0–500	1.00	
501–1,000	2.00	
1,001–5,000	5.00	These figures represent a
5,001–6,000	6.00	*Personal Application fee* only
6,001–7,000	7.00	No *Court Fee* is payable on
7,001–8,000	8.00	estates below £10,000.
8,001–9,000	9.00	
9,001–10,000	10.00	
10,001–25,000	£40.00 Court Fee *plus* £1.00 for every £1,000 net estate or part of £1,000 Personal Application Fee.	
25,001–40,000	£80.00 Court Fee *plus* £1.00 for every £1,000 net estate or part of £1,000 Personal Application Fee.	

40,001–70,000	£150.00 Court Fee *plus* £1.00 for every £1,000 net estate or part of £1,000 Personal Application Fee.
70,001–100,000	£215.00 Court Fee *plus* £1.00 for every £1,000 net estate or part of £1,000 Personal Application Fee.
100,001–200,000	£300.00 Court Fee *plus* £1.00 for every £1,000 net estate or part of £1,000 Personal Application Fee.
Over 200,000	£300.00 Court Fee for the first £200,000 *plus* £50.00 for every additional £100,000 net estate or part of £100,000 *plus* £1.00 for every £1,000 net estate or part of £1,000 Personal Application Fee.

Source: Crown copyright, reproduced with the permission of the Controller of HMSO (PA4)

Personal Applicants, Probate Fees Payable in England and Wales for deaths *after* 26 April 1999.

Under £5,000	Nil
£5,001 and over	£130

Index

absolute gift   22, 46
absolute interest   24–25
accountants   42
accounts   152–54
   capital   152–54, 155–56
   income   154
accumulation and
      maintenance settlements
      72, 84
Administration of Estates Act
      (1925)   30, 97
Administration of Justice Act
      (1970)   103
administrator   22, 32, 40,
      89
annuities   97
assent   143
asset(s)   16, 22, 34, 37, 76
   checklist   56–58
   disposal   82–83
   transfer between husband
      and wife   73
   valuation   114–29, 157
attestation clause   53, 60
attorney *see* solicitors

bank/building society accounts
      122
   in Scotland   131
banks   6, 42, 108
   as executors   40

executorship account   108,
      122, 150
   loans   56
beneficiary   16, 22, 63–64
   distribution of income to
      96–98
bequest   22
bond of caution   22, 131
Bonds and Stock Office   121
bookkeeping   144–46
business
   partnerships   66, 102
   property relief   79–80

capital accounts   152–54,
      155–56
capital gains tax   89, 91
capital taxation   14, 91
Capital Taxes Office   86, 93,
      110
   Scotland   139
capital transfer tax *see*
      inheritance tax
Chancery Court   55
chargeable gift   22
charities   75, 91
children   18, 22, 63–64
   adopted and illegitimate
      32, 135
   as sole beneficiaries   63–64
   Scotland   135–36

settlements   72–73, 84
step   135
Citizens Advice Bureau
    108
codicil   1, 14, 18, 22, 41, 49,
    53–54, 66–67
Commissary Office   94, 103,
    131, 139
    see also Scottish law
confirmation   22, 25
continuous family inheritance
    50
contrary to public policy
    50–51
council tax   116
Courts and Legal Services Act
    6
creditors   102
Crown   22, 28, 32, 105

death abroad   111
death certificate   110–11,
    115, 157
death charge   73
debts   77, 91, 102, 126–27,
    152
    Scotland   138–39
deceased   22
deed of family arrangement
    9, 77–78
deed of variation   77–78
deposit certificate   41
descendants   22
devise and bequeath   23, 64
disposing of an asset   82–83
distribution   23
    estate   154–56
    legacies   150–52
    sheet   154

District Valuer   116
divorce, effect on wills   32,
    48, 138
docket   23
documentation   110–13
    death certificate   110–11
domicile   74, 76–77
donor   23
    body organs   15, 35, 66,
        157
    cards   35, 66

endowment policy   36–37
engrossment   23
equalisation, of estate
    70–72, 84
estate   34
    administering   114–29
    checklist   133–34
    heritable   135
    moveable   135
    residue of   60, 97–98
    Scotland   130–39
    valuation   71–72, 84, 109,
        114–29
estate planning   11
excepted estates   43–45, 112,
    157
    in Scotland   45
executor   14, 15, 18, 23, 28,
    49
    and taxation   93
    bookkeeping   144–45
    dative   130, 135
    duties   39–40, 94, 144, 146
    expenses   40, 96, 150
    form of renunciation   40
    nominate   135
    sources of help   99–109

expenses
  as administrator 30, 96
  as executor 40, 96, 150
  as trustee 42

family income benefit 36
family trusts 100
Finance Act (1986) 72, 82
financial matters 35–39
  insurance policies 35–38
  money 38–39
form of
  nomination 34
  renunciation 40
freehold property 35, 144
funeral
  arrangements 14, 94
  expenses 77

gifts 51, 74–75
  and tax 68–69, 72
  charities 75
  making void 51
  political parties 75, 91
  public benefit/national
     purposes 75
  small 74
grant
  of probate 23, 105,
     111–13, 121, 157,
     158
  Representation 23, 25
guardianship 18

heritable property
  in Scotland 132, 135, 136
hire purchase *see* debts
holograph will 14, 53
home-made will 55

How to Obtain Probate (PA2)
  110
husband 23
  see *also* surviving spouse

income tax 94–96, 146
Individual Savings Accounts
  (ISAs) 38–39, 125–26
infant 23 *see also* children
inheritance, order of 31–32
Inheritance Act (1975) 8
Inheritance (Provision for
  Family and Dependants)
  Act (1975) 8, 49
inheritance tax 37, 56, 59,
  68–69
  allowable expenses 90–91
  application 76–77
  calculating 117
  forms 86, 112
  insurance against 88
  interest on 113
  penalties for late payment
    81
inheritance tax threshold 11,
  37, 38, 156
Inland Revenue 9, 11, 43,
  70, 77, 86–87, 148
  assessment for tax 89–90
  deed of variation 78
  District Valuer 116
  Scotland 133
  total income schedule 152
insolvency 100, 102
insurable interest 37
insurance policies 35,
  121–22, 131
  in Scotland 131
  inheritance tax 88

interest   24
  absolute   24–25
  life   24, 31
interest in possession trusts
    72, 83
intestacy   6–7, 10, 24, 27,
    101
  law   27–33
  Scotland   136–38
issue   24, 102

jewellery   109, 127
joint ownership   34, 85–86,
    143
joint tenant   24, 85

Law Reform (Succession) Act
    (1995)   8
Land Registry   141
  fees   142
Law Society   6, 101
  Code of Conduct   102
  complaints bureau   6
  Personal Assets Log   102
leasehold property   35,
    143–44
legacy/ies   24
  distributing   150–51
  general   96–97
  specific   97
  statutory   30, 31
legal rights
  in Scotland   24, 132–33,
    137
letter of renunciation   99
letters of administration   23,
    30, 105, 158
life insurance policy   35–36
  term insurance   38

whole of life insurance
    38
life interest   24, 27, 31, 39,
    45–46
  clauses in will   64
  tax position   98
life tenant   25, 42–43, 84
lifetime charge   73

marriage
  effect on wills   33, 47
  gifts in consideration of
    75
medical research, leaving your
    body to   66
Mental Health Act   15–16
money   38–39
Morgan Grenfell   11
mortgage   140, 141, 143
moveable property   25, 135

National Savings account
    34, 56, 105, 121, 152
  certificates   120
  in Scotland   132
next of kin   25
Non-Contentious Probate
    Rules   52–53

order
  of inheritance   31–32
  of succession   138
overdraft settlement   114–15

partnership agreement   66,
    102
pecuniary legacies   25,
    28–39, 60
pensions policy   37

personal
  assets log 102
  effects 30
  tax matters 89–98
Personal Equity Plans (PEPs)
  38–39, 125
personal representative 25,
  28–30, 40
political parties, gifts to, 75,
  91
potentially exempt transfer
  2, 69, 72
power of appointment 25
premium bonds 56, 120–21
  in Scotland 132
prior rights
  in Scotland 132–33, 137
probate 8, 25, 25
  checklist 157–58
  fees 104, 159–60
Probate Registry 27, 28–30,
  39 41, 43, 55, 56, 86–87,
  94, 103–09
  addresses 105–08
  appointment of
    administrator 40
  function 104
  grant of probate 111–13
  Personal Applications
    Department 8, 100,
    112
  tasks of 52–53
property 11, 34–35, 52,
  140–44
  business property relief
    79–80
  freehold 35, 144
  jointly owned 85–86
  leasehold 35, 143–44

  moveable 25
  overseas 15
  tax rules 80–82
  transferring ownership
    143
  valuation 116–20
Public Index Map 141

redirection of post 115
Registrar of Deeds 139
Registry for Births, Deaths
  and Marriages 110
residuary bequest 94
residue 25
revocation clause 59

Scotland *see* Scottish law
Scottish law 14, 24, 47, 53,
  130–39
  children 135–36
  estate checklist 133–34
  small estates 43
  see also Commissary Office
settlements 72–73, 93
  small discretionary 73
settlor 83
shares 38–39, 45, 79,
  80–82, 148
  in Scotland 132
  valuation 123–24
small estates 25, 43, 118
  Scotland 130–31
solicitors 42, 99, 101–102
  as executors 40
  charges 2, 101–02
Somerset House 41, 104,
  108
sound mind 16
stamp collections 115

stamp duty   139, 144–46
Stanley Gibbons   116
Statute of Limitations   50
statutory legacy   27, 30, 31
stocks *see* shares
Succession (Scotland) Act
   (1964)   137
surviving
  children   24, 63–64
  relatives   10, 30
  spouse   7, 24, 30, 31, 45,
    64, 86, 91–92
survivor   25
survivorship clause   60

tax   37, 68–88
  allowances   94
  codes   94
  consultant   108
  exemptions   73
  payment   86–87
  relief   77, 79–80
  returns   46, 93, 146–48
  Scotland   133
  self-assessment   89,
    92–94
  surviving spouse   91–92
  see also income tax;
    inheritance tax
tax planning   9, 70, 73
  deed of variation   77–78
Taxes Management Act
   (1970)   89–90
tenancy-in -common   25, 85,
   116
TESSAs   125
testamentary expenses   25,
   59
testator   14, 25

title deeds   140, 142, 143
Treasury Solicitor   104–05
trust   26, 28, 41–43, 72–73,
   95, 101
  administering   128–29
  discretionary   73, 85
  interest in possession
    83–84
  statutory   31
  tax planning   83
trustee   26, 28, 42, 93, 95

unit trusts   38–39, 124,
   148
Unlisted Securities Market
   (USM)   79
unregistered title   100

valuation of an estate   109,
   114–29, 157

*What Happens When Someone
   Dies?* (IR45)   92
wife 23
  common-law   32
  see also surviving spouse
will(s)
  aims   16–18
  and divorce   32, 48, 138
  and marriage   33, 47
  checklist   55–61
  disputes about   49–51
  example   61–63, 114
  home-made   55
  need for   10–26
  revoking a   48–49
  rules to follow   52–54
  validity   8
  where to keep it   40–41

who can make a   15–16
    wording   55
winding up an estate   140–56

wish of intent   49
witnesses   60–61, 66, 67
works of art register   11

Index of Advertisers

Aid for the Aged in Distress
vi–vii

British Council for the
Prevention of Blindness   v
British Trust for Ornithology
viii, 147
British Veterinary Association
153
British Wireless for the Blind
Fund   xi
BUAV   xiv

Cancer Prevention Research
Trust   12
Children's Heart Surgery Fund
viii

The Donkey Sanctuary   57

ITDG (Intermediate
Technology)   13

League Against Cruel Sports   3
Musicians Benevolent Fund
20–21

The Not Forgotten Association
28, 109

Royal British Legion   17, 145
RSPCA   ii

Salvation Army   xii
Seaman's Mission   7, 153
Shire Horse Society   24, 129
The Shaftesbury Society   4–5
SPANA   29, 151
SSAFA Forces Help   xvi–xviii
St Tiggywinkles – The Wildlife
Hospital Trust   viii

Wood Green Animal Shelters
xv, 149

Yorkshire Wildlife Trust   19